INU YASHA

The popular anime series now on DVD—each season available in a collectible box set

TV SERIES & MOVIES ON DVD!

See more of the action in _Inuyasha_ full-length movies

INUYASHA

Read the action from the start with the original manga series

Full color adaptation of the popular TV series

Art book with cel art, paintings, character profiles and more

Gosho Aoyama's
Mystery Library

35

DRURY LANE

Disguise is a crucial detective skill, and Drury Lane is a master! A retired Shakespearean actor, he leads a life of ease, but his curiosity leads him to investigate puzzling cases. As an actor, he finds disguises a piece of cake. With his assistant Quacey helping him with makeup, he disguises himself as a police inspector or a suspect. He connects the information he gathers in a logical, mathematical way. He's deaf, but this works to his advantage, since he can concentrate perfectly by closing his eyes.

Drury's adventures were written by Barnaby Ross, a pseudonym of cousins Frederic Dannay and Manfred Lee, a.k.a. Ellery Queen. When the Drury Lane books were first published, Dannay and Lee decided to use a new pen name, and their fans were completely deceived. It's like the time I wrote a manga about a palm-sized detective...except I used my real name. Guess I was too obvious.

I recommend *The Tragedy of Y*.

[Editor's Note: The manga Aoyama refers to is the untranslated miniseries *Tantei Jorji's Minimini-Daisakusen* (Detective George's Mini-Mini Operations).]

Hello, Aoyama here.

I played in a baseball game recently. I hadn't played baseball in four years!

The opposing team was the Whiters, led by sports-manga superstar Tetsuya Chiba! After several foul balls, I managed to get a decent hit. I ran to first base, which was defended by the great Chiba. ♥ I was really hoping to talk to him, but my teammates called in a pinch runner to take my place since I'm so flabby, so the conversation ended there.

Stay in shape, everybody!

[Editor's note: Tetsuya Chiba is a legendary manga artist best known for the boxing manga *Ashita no Joe* (Joe of Tomorrow).]

ARRGH... CRUD...

KCH

KCH

WILL YA TWO SHUT YER YAPS?

YEAH, THE OTHERS GOT BACK AN HOUR AGO.

HEY, I WONDER WHAT'S TAKING TAIRA SO LONG.

DAKKA

?!

MAYBE SHE WENT OUT FOR THAT LATE DIVE.

MAYBE...

...

THE PRINCESS SLEEPS IN THE *KO* AND NOT IN THE *OTSU*...

OF COURSE NOT!

YOU'RE NOT PRETENDIN' TA BE STUMPED SO YOU CAN HELP TOKYO WIN, ARE YA?

NO, NOTH-ING.

HEY, KUDO, YA FIGURED ANYTHING OUT?

IT MEANS THE PRINCESS IS SLEEPIN' IN *NUMBER ONE* AND NOT *NUMBER TWO.*

KO, OTSU AND *HEI* ARE OLD RANKING TERMS: FIRST, SECOND, THIRD...

NO, HANG ON!

MAYBE IT MEANS, "THE PRINCESS IS NUMBER ONE WHEN SHE'S ASLEEP!"

...

HA! ♥

GOOD ONE!

LIKE THAT OLD SAYING, "DON'T KNOW WHICH IS *KO* AND WHICH IS *OTSU*."

MAYBE IT MEANS, "THE PRINCESS IS NUMBER ONE, BUT SHE DOESN'T LOOK THAT NICE WHEN SHE'S SLEEPIN'!"

I FEEL LIKE URASHIMA TARO.*

YEAH, IT LOOKED COMPLETELY DIFFERENT LAST TIME I WAS HERE.

I KNEW IT! WHITE!

...BUT IT GOT TORN APART BY THE TYPHOON. THEY ONLY RECENTLY FIXED IT.

IT USED TO BE RENTED OUT AS A VACATION COTTAGE...

*A Japanese folk hero similar to Rip van Winkle.

THIS AREA'S A GREAT PLACE TO CATCH AMBER-STRIPE SCAD.

YEAH... UNTIL ABOUT TWO YEARS AGO, I USED TO WATCH THIS ISLAND FROM MY SHIP.

LAST TIME... DID YOU COME HERE OFTEN?

BUT AFTER THEY FOUND THE BODY A LOT OF OUR FRIENDS STOPPED COMING. THEY SAID IT WAS TOO CREEPY.

YEAH. THERE'S A GREAT DIVING SPOT A LITTLE PAST THE ISLAND.

YOU GUYS KNOW THIS PLACE TOO, RIGHT?

AMBER-STRIPE SCAD?

?

THIS GUY DOESN'T REALLY THINK WE CAN CRACK THE CASE, DOES HE?

OKAY!

ANYTHING THAT LOOKS MYSTERIOUS OR SPOOKY!

OKAY! I'LL BE HERE DISCUSSING THE SPECIAL WITH HARLEY. YOU SCOUT AROUND THE ISLAND FOR LOCATIONS!

THE PRINCESS SLEEPS IN THE KO AND NOT IN THE OTSU

"...IN THE *KO* AND NOT IN THE *OTSU*."

"THE PRINCESS SLEEPS..."

IT WAS A YEAR AGO. THE MAN HAD DIED FROM LACK OF FOOD OR WATER.

THE CORPSE WAS LEANING HERE WITH ITS BACK TO THE CARVING.

THAT'S RIGHT.

THEY FOUND THE BODY IN FRONT OF THIS PILLAR?

...SO THE LOCALS THINK HE WAS FROM THE CREW OF A BOAT THAT SANK NEAR HERE.

AROUND THAT TIME, A SERIES OF HUGE TYPHOONS SWEPT THIS AREA...

THE PRINCESS SLEEPS IN THE KO AND NOT IN THE OTSU

MR. KANE-SHIRO, THE MAYOR.

WHO BUILT A *HOUSE* ON THIS DESERTED ISLAND?

HEY...

...

BUT THIS STRANGE CARVING...

...

HEY, CAPTAIN! DON'T MAKE SO MANY WAVES!

...

HR AAH

HUH... THAT'S FUNNY.

TRY A **BLACK WETSUIT**, HARLEY.

UH... YEAH...

SPLISH

BETTER GET TO WORK!

THE DIRECTOR'S CALLING YOU!

HARLEY!!

I HEARD THE SEA AROUND THIS ISLAND IS...

HMM ...

THAT DIDN'T COME OUT QUITE RIGHT...

...SO *HANDS OFF!!*

...MY LOUD-MOUTHED, NO-GOOD CHILDHOOD FRIEND I BARELY KNOW...

HE'S ONE OF OUR FEATURED GUESTS!

HARLEY HARTWELL, THE SLEUTH OF THE WEST.

YOSHIE TAIRA (26) CREW

WHAT'RE YOU DOING ON THIS BOAT? YOU'RE NOT ON THE CREW, ARE YOU?

HUH? DONCHA KNOW ME?

SO WHO ARE YOU?

THAT'S WHAT MAKES IT A GREAT STORY!

BUT HE'S JUST A KID!

THIS GUY?

LET'S GET THIS OVER WITH AND HEAD BACK.

WHATEVER.

HEY, *HE* CHALLENGED *ME!*

THE ROOKIE TEEN DETECTIVE CHALLENGING RICHARD MOORE!

WE KNOW A GREAT SPOT!

WHY DON'T WE GO FOR A SWIM TOGETHER AFTER THE SHOOT TOMORROW?

I'M FROM OSAKA!

THAT'S RIGHT.

TOKYO?

WHERE ARE YOU FROM?

NOBURO IKEMA (24) CREW

YOSHITSUGU KUME (25) CREW

THESE CHICKS'RE BOOKED TODAY, TOMORROW AN' THE DAY AFTER!

NO WAY!

...WEARIN' PENGUIN FLIPPERS AN' TUBES IN OUR MOUTHS! SO *SCRAM!*

UNLIKE YOU GUYS, WE AIN'T GOT TIME TO SPLASH AROUND IN THE WATER...

HIS WHAT?

NO! SHE'S MY...

YOU THIS GIRL'S *BROTHER* OR SOMETHING?

HUH?

FUNAURA ISLAND, WHERE THEY FOUND THE UNIDENTIFIED BODY!

SHOOO

THERE IT IS!

CHECK IT OUT! THE TIP OF THE ISLAND LOOKS LIKE A TURTLE'S HEAD!

LOCALS CALL IT ONIGAME... "DEMON TURTLE"!

SAY WHAT?

SHOOO

IT'S A PLAN FOR REVIVIN' THE ISLANDS.

HARLEY, WHY'D YOU AGREE TO THIS STUPID DEDUCTION MATCH AGAINST MR. MOORE?

THE REST OF THE FILM CREW IS JUST LOCALS WHO KNOW THE SEA AN' THE ISLANDS.

ANYHOW, THE ONLY PROFESSIONAL TV GUY HERE IS MR. TAKETOMI.

THE MAYOR RUNS BOTH THE ISLANDS HERE.

I DON'T THINK FOOTAGE OF A DEAD BODY IS GOING TO IMPROVE THEIR IMAGE WITH TOURISTS...

MR. KANESHIRO, THE MAYOR, SAID THEY'VE HAD SERIOUS TROUBLE WITH CRIME, LIKE KIDNAPPINGS AN' ROBBERIES. THE TOURIST TRADE'S DRIED UP, SO NOW THEY'RE TRYIN' TA IMPROVE THEIR IMAGE WITH THIS TV SPECIAL!

THAT DESERTED ISLAND WHERE THE *CORPSE* AND *MESSAGE* WERE DISCOVERED.

THAT'S RIGHT. WE'RE MAKING A RUN TO THE ISLAND YOU AND MR. MOORE WILL BE VISITING TOMORROW!

REHEARSAL?

MASAO TAKETOMI (43) TV DIRECTOR

IT AIN'T FAIR TA GET A HEAD START...

WELL...

...SLEUTH OF THE WEST?

WANT TO JOIN US...

HEY!

SURE! I'LL TAG ALONG!

...BUT IT'LL *TICK ME OFF* IF KUDO HELPS THE OL' MAN SOLVE THE MYSTERY AHEAD A' ME...

?

I'M FROM TOKYO, YOU KNOW...

...AN' PROVE TO THE AUDIENCE ONCE AN' FER ALL THAT TOKYO FOLKS AIN'T GOT NOTHIN' ON OSAKANS!

WE CAN SOLVE THE CASE TOGETHER RIGHT NOW...

I BET YER MOM AN' DAD WOULD JUST LOVE TO HEAR ABOUT *THIS* ONE.

TEACHIN' A GRADE-SCHOOL KID TO OGLE WOMEN?

KA... KAZUHA...

TIGER STRIPES?

HEY!!

HARLEY'S ON A ROLL TODAY! HE GUESSED YOU'D BE WEARING A SWIMSUIT WITH TIGER STRIPES!

IT AIN'T MY FAULT! THE KID BEGGED ME TA PLAY! I JUST WENT ALONG!

THEY'RE *ZEBRA* STRIPES! ZEBRA!

DO THESE LOOK LIKE TIGER STRIPES TO YOU?

*Osaka's baseball team, the Hanshin Tigers, is famous for having the most devoted fans in the league.

WOULD I GET MAD JUST 'CAUSE SOME LOSER LEFT ME HANGIN' FOR FOUR HOURS?

GET SERI-OUS!

DON'T TELL ME YER STILL MAD AT ME FOR KEEPIN' YA WAITIN' AT BIG MAN IN UMEDA!

SPLASH

ER... RIGHT...

TIGER'S

AN' THE *TIGER'S* THE ONLY STRIPED ANIMAL IN OSAKA!*

WHAT-EVER! IT'S A ZOO ANIMAL, AIN'T IT?

FILE 11:
DEA

ISLAND

'KAY, WHAT ABOUT THE BLONDE BABE OVER THERE?

FILE 11: DEATH.ISLAND

NAH... SHE'S A LITTLE ON THE CHUBBY SIDE, SO SHE'S WEARIN' A *BLACK BIKINI* THAT MAKES HER LOOK THINNER.

HMM... SHE'S LETTING HER ROOTS SHOW, SO SHE DOESN'T CARE MUCH ABOUT HER LOOKS. I SAY A MODEST ONE-PIECE SWIMSUIT.

BACK OFF...

YA SURE SUCK AT THESE KINDSA DEDUCTIONS, KUDO.

WHO SUCKS, HARLEY?

WHAT'D I TELL YA? I WIN AGAIN!

SPLSH

THAT'S IT! THEY WENT ON TO THE NEXT NEWS THING, SO I DON'T KNOW WHAT IT LOOKS LIKE. BUT DON'T YOU WANNA SEE IT, ANITA?

YEAH, SURE.

THE TSUCHI-NOKO? IT'S A MYTHICAL MONSTER.

TSUCHI-NOKO...

TSU...

...

HEY, I'M GOING TO SEE MY UNCLE IN GIFU SOON...

IF I REMEMBER CORRECTLY, IT'S BEEN SPOTTED IN GIFU, OKA-YAMA AND HYOGO.

DON'T BOTHER.

GOT A PROBLEM WITH THAT?

HEY! YOU'RE GONNA TRY TO FIND ONE AND SHOW IT OFF TO THE GIRLS!

YOU DID IT FOR US?

WHAT? AW, MITCH...

...ON OUR WAY BACK FROM THE FIRE-WORKS!

AMY AND ANITA MENTIONED THEY WANTED TO SEE A FIREFLY...

IT WAS REALLY PRETTY!!

THANK YOU!

I'M NOT SURE.

BUT WHY DID NUMABUCHI BRING MITCH BACK TO US? HE KNEW HE'D BE CAUGHT!

...AND HE JUST WANTED TO COME BACK ONE LAST TIME BEFORE HIS EXECUTION.

IT COULD BE THAT HIS STORY ABOUT BURYING A FOURTH BODY IN THIS FOREST WAS A LIE...

IF HE'D BEEN EAVESDROPPING ON OUR CONVERSATION, HE MIGHT'VE REALIZED MITCH HAD GOTTEN LOST LOOKING FOR FIREFLIES. WHEN HE SAW MITCH WITH HIS HANDS CLASPED TOGETHER, HE WOULD'VE KNOWN FOR SURE.

REALLY?

MAYBE HE CAME HERE FOR THE SAME REASON AS MITCH.

...WHICH WAS WHY HE ACCIDENTALLY BOUGHT AN ADULT TICKET!

YEAH. AND HE PRESSED THE SAME BUTTON THEY PRESSED ON THE TICKET MACHINE AT THE STATION...

I SEE... HE WAS LOOKING STRAIGHT AHEAD ON THE BUS BECAUSE HE DIDN'T WANT TO LOSE SIGHT OF THE MEN HE WAS TAILING.

MITCH DECIDED TO FOLLOW THE MEN TO FIND FIREFLIES.

THOSE ARE ALL NOBLE CLANS THAT FOUGHT EACH OTHER.

THE GIRL AT THE FLOWER SHOP MENTIONED THE NAMES UESUGI AND TAKADA, TOYOTOMI AND TOKUGAWA.

BUT WHAT ABOUT THE NAMES OF THE LORDS?

HE WANTED TO USE THE BAMBOO LEAVES TO LINE AN INSECT CAGE TO CARRY THE FIREFLIES HOME. THEY LIKE BROAD, FLAT LEAVES.

WHAT ABOUT THE BAMBOO DUMPLINGS?

...AND "GENJI" AND "HEIKE" ARE TWO SPECIES OF JAPANESE FIREFLY!

OTHER FAMOUS CLANS THAT FOUGHT ARE THE HEIAN CLANS GENJI AND HEIKE...

BUT IF HE'D TOLD US, IT WOULDN'T HAVE BEEN A SURPRISE!

HMPH... IF YOU WANTED TO CATCH BUGS, YOU SHOULD'VE TOLD US!

ISN'T THAT RIGHT, MITCH?

EVEN WHEN HE REALIZED WE WERE LOOKING FOR HIM, HE DIDN'T WANT TO OPEN HIS HANDS AND LET THE FIREFLY GO.

HE MANAGED TO CATCH A FIREFLY, BUT THEN HE GOT LOST IN THE FOREST.

...YOU DON'T SEE IN THE CITY!

THAT'S RIGHT. AN IMAGE OF SUMMER...

A FIRE-FLY?

FIRE-FLIES CAN ONLY LIVE NEAR CLEAN WATER.

MITCH KEPT ASKING THEM WHERE HE COULD FIND FIRE-FLIES. THEY WERE UPSET BECAUSE THEY DIDN'T WANT CHILDREN DISRUPTING THE FOREST THEY WORKED SO HARD TO PRESERVE.

...WERE *ECOLO-GISTS* WHO COME DOWN TO THIS FOREST TO LOOK AFTER THE FIREFLY ENVIRON-MENT.

THE MEN TALKING TO MITCH AT THE BUS STOP...

COME TO THINK OF IT, WHEN HE WAS ARRESTED, THE TV CAMERAS CAUGHT HIM SHOUTING SOMETHING LIKE, "IT'S ALL THEIR FAULT!"

THEN AGAIN... IF HE KILLED SOMEONE BEFORE HE JOINED THE SYNDICATE, HE'S HARDLY PURE AS THE DRIVEN SNOW.

SINCE THEN, THE POOR FOOL'S KILLED *THREE PEOPLE*, THINKING THEY WERE ASSASSINS SENT BY THE SYNDICATE.

HE MUST HAVE PANICKED WHEN HE REALIZED HE WAS IN OVER HIS HEAD.

WAIT A MINUTE.

HE'S BEEN SENTENCED TO DEATH, SO—

THAT'S RIGHT... BUT IT JUST SOUNDED LIKE THE RAVINGS OF A MADMAN. SINCE HE NEVER KNEW ANYTHING ABOUT THE INNER WORKINGS OF THE SYNDICATE, THEY DECIDED TO LET THE POLICE TAKE CARE OF HIM.

HUH?

IT WORRIES ME.

YOU'RE RIGHT. I DIDN'T SENSE ANYTHING.

WHY DIDN'T YOU NOTICE NUMABUCHI HIDING IN THE TREE?

YOU ONCE TOLD ME YOU COULD PICK OUT THE MEN IN BLACK. YOU SAID THEY HAD A CERTAIN *SMELL*.

I'M REALLY USELESS, AREN'T I?

BUT I'M STARTING TO LOSE IT. I'VE GOTTEN COMPLACENT.

IT WAS THE ONLY WAY I COULD STAY AHEAD OF THEM.

IN THE PAST, I COULD EVEN PICK UP THAT SCENT ON MY *SISTER*.

THE SYNDICATE TOOK INTEREST IN HIS NATURAL AGILITY. THEY WANTED TO TRAIN HIM TO BE A SKILLED ASSASSIN.

BUT HE WAS ONLY ON THE OUTERMOST FRINGE OF THE ORGANIZATION.

ZHK

ZHK

BUT HE DISAPPOINTED THEM, SO THEY SENT HIM TO ME...

WHY'D HE RUN?

I ESCAPED MYSELF SOON AFTER THAT, SO WE'VE NEVER MET IN PERSON.

BUT HE MADE A RUN FOR IT BEFORE WE COULD TEST THE DRUG ON HIM.

THAT'S WHY I KNOW SO MUCH ABOUT HIM. THEY SENT ME ALL HIS MEDICAL DATA SO I COULD COMPARE IT TO HIS CONDITION AFTER THE TESTS.

WHAT?

...TO USE AS A *HUMAN GUINEA PIG* FOR MY NEW DRUG.

DAKKA

HIS BACK IS CROOKED, BUT HE'S AGILE, LIKE AN ANIMAL.

HE'S GAUNT, WITH A TURNED-UP NOSE. HIS FACE LOOKS LIKE IT'S PASTED DIRECTLY TO HIS SKULL.

THAT'S RIGHT.

DON'T TELL ME HE'S...

ANITA... HOW DO YOU KNOW SO MUCH ABOUT THIS MAN?

THEN WE HAFTA LOOK FOR A GUY WHO LOOKS LIKE A SKELETON?

I GUESS SO...

NUMABUCHI IS A FORMER MEMBER OF THE SYNDICATE.

...YOU'RE AFTER.

HE'S ONE OF THE MEN IN BLACK...

BUT HE COULD STILL CALL US WITH HIS BADGE!

OH NO...

...HE COULD'VE LOST HIS VOICE.

IF HE GOT LOST EARLY IN THE DAY AND WAS CALLING FOR HELP FOR HOURS...

BUT HE COULD'VE DONE THAT ONLY IF HE WAS ABLE TO USE HIS *HANDS!*

RIGHT... IF HE'D USED HIS BADGE, WE'D HAVE FOUND HIM BY NOW!

WE'LL JUST LOOK FOR THE KILLER TOO!

BUT WHAT IF HE'S HURT? WHAT IF HE GOT CAPTURED BY THE KILLER? HOW WILL WE FIND HIM?

NOW, NOW! WE CAN WORRY ABOUT THAT LATER!

IF HE'S IN THIS AREA, WE'D BETTER START LOOKING!

WHAT'S WRONG WITH HIS HANDS?

HUH?

FINE EYEBROWS. HOLLOW EYES.

LET ME SEE... THE DESCRIPTION OF NUMABUCHI ON THE NEWS WAS...

IT WAS TOO DARK TO SEE HIS FACE. I'LL MIX HIM UP WITH ALL THE POLICEMEN.

DID THAT *KILLER* FIND HIM?

...

MITCH... OH NO...

HE DIDN'T STOP TO PICK IT UP. THIS COULD BE A SERIOUS SITUATION.

LOOK, IT'S THE CAP I BORROWED FROM MITCH THE OTHER DAY AT THE SOCCER GAME.

YES, SIR!

CONTACT THE OTHER SEARCH SQUADS AND TELL THEM TO BE CARE-FUL. THE SUSPECT MAY HAVE TAKEN A CHILD HOSTAGE!

W... WE'D BETTER SEARCH THE AREA!

HE WAS HERE MOMENTS AGO.

THE SWEAT ON THIS CAP HASN'T DRIED, AND IT'S STILL A LITTLE WARM.

NO. HE HASN'T GONE FAR.

WHAT SHOULD WE DO NOW? IF MITCH IS RUNNING AWAY FROM NUMABUCHI, HE COULD BE ANY-WHERE...

MITCH PROBABLY ARRIVED AT THE FOREST BEFORE NOON. WE GOT HERE AROUND DUSK.

HUH?

I BET HE CAN'T RAISE HIS VOICE.

WHY DIDN'T HE SHOUT BACK?

BUT YOU KEPT SHOUTING FOR HIM, DIDN'T YOU, CONAN?

HE RAN OFF INTO THE WOODS!

HE'D CLIMBED UP A TREE LIKE A MONKEY! WHEN WE SPOTTED HIM HE JUMPED DOWN!

IN A TREE!

SIGH... WELL, WHERE WAS HE HIDING?

I FIGURED OUT WHERE MITCH IS!

I WASN'T GOING AFTER HIM!

THEN CONAN RAN OFF AFTER HIM ON HIS OWN...

HA HA HA...

MR. YAMA?

RIGHT, MR. YAMA?

HE'S SOME-WHERE ALONG THIS STREAM!!

LOOKS LIKE YOU'RE RIGHT. HE *WAS* HERE... BUT THAT'S AS FAR AS YOUR DEDUCTION WILL TAKE US.

WHAT?

NO! I FIGURED IT OUT BE-CAUSE—

TREA-SURE?

WHY IS HE THERE?

STREAM?

MY... MY FRIEND GOT LOST IN HERE.

I THOUGHT YAMA-MURA WAS GOING TO ESCORT YOU OUT OF THE FOREST.

OH, HI, SIR...

HEY! YOU'RE THAT KID WHO WAS TALKING TO YAMA-MURA!

SIR!!

DAKKA

OH?

I'VE FOUND KIICHIRO NUMA-BUCHI!!

HUH?

BUT I'VE GOT BIG NEWS!!

ER... UM... POOR TIMING?

WHY DIDN'T YOU TELL ME A KID WAS LOST IN THIS FOREST?

YOU SERIOUSLY THINK I COULD GET HIM ON MY OWN? HE RAN AWAY THE MOMENT I SAW HIM.

WELL? WHERE IS HE? YOU APPREHENDED HIM, RIGHT?

REALLY?

WHAT?

FILE 10:
MISSING MITCH ③

BUT I'VE FIGURED OUT WHAT THE SCENT OF LEMON IS!

I HAVE NO IDEA WHAT THAT MEANS.

MITCH CAME HERE WITH A BACKPACK FULL OF BAMBOO DUMPLINGS. AND HE SMELLED LIKE LEMON!

SOME MEN WERE SCOLDING MITCH AND MENTIONED THE NAMES OF OLD FEUDAL LORDS.

WHAT?

THEY'RE FRAGRANCES OFTEN USED AS *INSECT REPELLENTS.*

IT MUST BE LEMON-GRASS OR CITRO-NELLA.

THAT MEANS HE WAS PLANNING TO COME OUT TO THE FOREST FROM THE START.

I SEE. MITCH BORROWED THE LOTION NOT TO PROTECT HIMSELF FROM THE SUN, BUT TO KEEP BUGS AWAY.

REMEMBER WHAT MITCH'S SISTER SAID? MITCH BORROWED SUNTAN LOTION SHE'D ORDERED IN THE MAIL! IT'S NOT THAT POPULAR IN JAPAN, BUT LOTS OF FOREIGN SUNTAN LOTIONS ALSO CONTAIN INSECT REPELLENT.

OH YES?

HUH?

MAYBE IT'S MOMOTARO, THE FAIRY TALE HERO! *HE* CARRIES DUMPLINGS!

BUT WHAT ABOUT THE OTHER CLUES? THE DUMPLINGS AND THE NAMES OF LORDS...

YOU'LL BE FINE! THE WATER'S VERY CLEAN. I DRANK FROM THIS STREAM ALL THE TIME WHEN I WAS LITTLE.

YEAH. I JUST GOT A LITTLE WET.

ARE YOU OKAY?

HEY, A STREAM.

IT'S COLD!

WHAT?

HUH?

GREAT... UNTIL YOU LET HIM ESCAPE.

NUMABUCHI AND I REALLY BONDED OVER IT...

YOU SEE, I USED TO PLAY IN THIS FOREST TOO.

THERE ARE THREE CLUES!

AH, WELL... I DON'T KNOW IF IT'S A CLUE OR NOT, BUT...

HOW CAN WE FIND YOUR BOY WITHOUT A SINGLE CLUE?

BUT WHAT NOW?

...AND BAMBOO DUMPLINGS!

...THE NAMES OF LORDS...

THE SCENT OF LEMON...

ANITA!

OR MAYBE HE'S ALREADY DEAD.

MAYBE HE FELL ASLEEP.

NOPE.

HASN'T MITCH PICKED UP YET?

BEEP

BEEP

HE SAID HE BURIED THE BODY IN THIS FOREST, NEAR HIS MOTHER'S HOMETOWN.

NO, *FOUR.* DURING QUESTIONING HE STARTED TO CLAIM HE'D KILLED SOMEONE ELSE FIRST.

I'VE HEARD OF HIM TOO. HE'S A SERIAL KILLER WHO'S KILLED THREE PEOPLE.

THE CRIMINAL LOOSE IN THIS FOREST IS KIICHIRO NUMABUCHI, WHO KILLED PEOPLE IN COLD BLOOD IN THE TOHOKU, KANTO AND KINKI REGIONS. IT'S A LOGICAL ASSESSMENT, ISN'T IT?

YOU KNOW THE CASE?

BUT NUMABUCHI'S MEMORIES WERE VAGUE, AND WE COULDN'T FIND A BODY.

THAT'S WHY WE BROUGHT HIM DOWN FROM OSAKA AND STARTED COMBING THE AREA.

EEK!

HE TOLD US ALL ABOUT HOW HE USED TO PLAY IN THE FOREST ALONE WHILE HIS MOTHER WAS AWAY...

BUT IT DIDN'T SEEM THAT WAY AT ALL.

I BET THAT'S WHAT HE WAS PLANNING ALL ALONG!

...ESCAPED, HUH?

WHEN THE DETECTIVES FROM OSAKA LEFT MY SUPERIOR AND ME WITH NUMABUCHI AND WENT TO GET A BITE TO EAT, HE...

HFF

HFF

ITS BEEPING AGAIN.

BEEP

BEEP

BEEP

BEEP

...MY WHOLE REASON FOR COMING HERE!

BUT IF I ANSWER NOW, IT'LL DESTROY...

I KNEW IT! THEY CAME LOOKING FOR ME!!

IT'S CONAN.

BEEP

I CAN'T ANSWER THAT CALL!!

NO!

...AND THE CASE IN KASHIRA-GAMI FOREST TOO. YOU WERE OUTSTANDING! REMEMBER?

...AND THAT CASE IN KARUI-ZAWA...

THE CASE WITH MR. YABUU-CHI...

YOU'VE HELPED SOLVE *LOTS* OF CASES BEFORE!!

WHAT?

THOUGH ALL THOSE CASES WERE *REALLY* SOLVED BY MY DAD OR ME...

WOW!!

HE WAS?

NO. FROM NOW ON...

PULL YOURSELF TOGETHER AND HELP US FIND MITCH! YOU KNOW THIS FOREST BETTER THAN WE DO, DETECTIVE YAMAMURA!

YOU THINK SO?

THE COP WITH THE BRAINS.

PLUS YOU HAVE A *REALLY BIG FOREHEAD*, SO YOU LOOK SMART!

*"Yama-san" is a common nickname for a veteran detective in old Japanese TV dramas.

HE WATCHES TOO MUCH TV...

MR. YAMA?

...CALL ME MR. YAMA.*

WHY DIDN'T YOU TELL THE COPS?

WE TOLD *YOU*, DIDN'T WE?

IT...

IT'S OVER.

THMP.

GEEZ.

I LEFT MY CELL PHONE IN THE POLICE CAR!!

SHOOT!

HUH...

I... I'LL CALL MY SUPERIOR...

...AND DIDN'T ALERT THE FORCE ABOUT A LOST CHILD. THEY'LL SACK ME FOR SURE.

I LET A DANGEROUS CRIMINAL ESCAPE...

THAT'S NOT TRUE!

...FOR THIS JOB...

I WORKED SO HARD TO BECOME A DETECTIVE BECAUSE I LOVE MYSTERY TV SHOWS.

BUT MAYBE I WAS NEVER SUITED...

IF YOU'RE HIDING, COME OUT!!

WHERE ARE YOU?

HEY, MITCH!!

WE'VE GOT *THESE*!

WE'RE OKAY IN THE DARK!

YOU SHOULD GO HOME TOO! I KNOW THIS FOREST WELL, BUT EVEN I CAN GET LOST IN THE DARK HERE...

PAF

PAF

I BET THE LITTLE BOY HAS ALREADY GONE HOME!

C'MON, GIVE IT UP!

MITCH!!

DOC AGASA MADE THEM FOR US!

WE DIDN'T BUY 'EM!

WOW... YOU CAN BUY PRETTY NIFTY TOYS THESE DAYS.

OF COURSE IT'S TRUE! THAT'S WHY WE'RE HERE!

THEN... THIS STORY ABOUT THE BOY LOST IN THE FOREST...

THE TRANS-MITTER BADGE AND RADAR GLASSES TOO!

THAT'S RIGHT. I INVENTED THEM FOR THE CHILDREN!

HE DID?

OOPS!

UM... THE BATTERY'S KIND OF DEAD...

IT'S JUST AN ORDINARY PAIR OF GLASSES.

THE BATTERY RAN OUT!

OH NO!

KLIK KLIK

BUT... THESE KIDS...

WE'RE STARTING THE SEARCH FOR NUMABUCHI!

HEY, YAMAMURA! WHAT'RE YOU DOING?

YES, SIR! VERY WELL!

ONCE YOU GET THOSE CHILDREN TO A SAFE PLACE, COME BACK AND JOIN THE SEARCH!

BUT SIR, I DIDN'T MEAN TO...

GET SERIOUS, WILL YOU?

THE KILLER ESCAPED BECAUSE *YOU* TOOK YOUR EYES OFF HIM!

...THAT'S *ONE* WAY TO PUT IT...

WELL...

SO YOU *WERE* THE ONE WHO LET HIM ESCAPE.

I HAD MY GUARD DOWN BECAUSE I THOUGHT I HAD BACKUP.

HMPH... NUMABUCHI ESCAPED BECAUSE *THAT GUY* LEFT HIS POST TO TAKE A LEAK IN THE BUSHES.

HUH?

ERASABLE MARKER PENS, CARDS THAT GIVE OFF SMOKE WHEN YOU RUB THEM...

OH... MY FOLKS GOT ME ONE OF THOSE DETECTIVE KITS WHEN I WAS LITTLE TOO!

RADAR GLAS-SES?

DETECTIVE BADGE?

...HOW WOULD THOSE THINGS HELP IN AN ACTUAL INVESTIGA-TION?

BUT ONE DAY, I SUDDENLY WON-DERED...

MITCH IS SOMEWHERE IN THIS FOREST!

HUH?

IT'S REALLY TRUE!

BUT WE'RE NOT PLAYING AROUND!

WELL, IF YOU WANT TO PLAY DETECTIVE WITH YOUR LITTLE TOYS, PLEASE DO IT ELSE-WHERE!

SEE, IF YOU PRESS THE BUTTON ON THE SIDE HERE...

FINE! SHOW ME THESE *RADAR GLASSES* OF YOURS!

KUK

THAT'S RIGHT.

WITH A *MURDERER* ON THE LOOSE?

WHAT? THERE'S A CHILD IN THE FOREST?

NO, NO, I DIDN'T!

AND AFTER *YOU* BROUGHT HIM OUT HERE!

HOW COULD YOU TAKE YOUR EYES OFF HIM?

I USED MY RADAR GLASSES!

THEN WE FOLLOWED THE TRANSMITTER ON HIS DETECTIVE BADGE AND ENDED UP HERE!

WE ASKED AROUND THE TRAIN STATIONS AND TRACKED HIM HERE TO GUNMA!

MITCH CAME HERE WITHOUT TELLING US!

...KIICHIRO NUMA-BUCHI!

THE MASS MUR-DERER...

WHAT?

WH...

WE'VE GOT TO WARN MITCH RIGHT AWAY!

HEY, CONAN!

BUT THERE'S A...

YOU HAVE TO GO!

THE GUY WHO STABBED ME IN OSAKA.

WHY WON'T HE PICK UP?

NUTS!!

BEEP

BEEP

BEEP
BEEP
B

HFF
HFF

LOOKS LIKE HE'S SOMEWHERE IN THIS FOREST.

LET'S ASK THEM IF THEY'VE SEEN MITCH!

LOOK! A BUNCH OF PEOPLE!!

I'M PRETTY SURE HIS BADGE IS RECEIVING MY CALLS, BUT...

HAVEN'T YOU GOTTEN IN TOUCH WITH HIM YET?

OH...

HEY!

HUH?

TAP

THIS MYSTERY MAY HAVE A PERFECTLY INNOCENT EXPLANATION!

NOW, NOW! LET'S NOT GET TOO SERIOUS!

MAYBE HE HAD A *REASON* FOR RUNNING AWAY...

THIS IS THE FIRST TIME HE'S EVER DITCHED THE GROUP... AND IT LOOKS LIKE HE DOESN'T WANT TO BE FOUND.

MITCH IS AN EARNEST, COOPERATIVE BOY.

LOVE AT FIRST SIGHT?

...AFTER FALLING IN LOVE AT FIRST SIGHT.

MAYBE HE FOLLOWED A GIRL HERE...

...THAT YOUR FIRST LOVE TASTES OF LEMON?

YOU KNOW THAT OLD JAPANESE SAYING...

BEEP

BEEP

B DETECTIVE BOYS

COME ON...

YEAH, RIGHT! LET'S MOVE OUT.

BUT NOW IT'S GETTING DARK.

WE MADE IT THIS FAR WITH JUST THE CAP, THE BACKPACK AND THE SCENT OF LEMON.

WHEW...

YEAH. UNLIKE THE TOKYO STATIONS, THIS STATION DOESN'T HAVE AN AUTOMATIC TICKET GATE. THE STATION STAFF SAW MITCH EXIT.

SO WE'RE IN GUNMA. YOU THINK MITCH GOT OFF HERE?

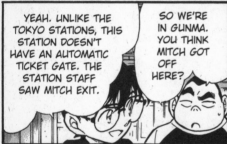

HE'S GOT TO BE AROUND HERE SOME-WHERE!

PIP

AND I'M GETTING A READING FROM HIS BADGE.

DOESN'T THIS SEEM PECULIAR?

BUT WITH MY RADAR GLASSES, I'LL BE ABLE TO TRACK HIM DOWN...

I'VE BEEN TRYING! HE WON'T ANSWER!

IF MITCH HAS HIS BADGE, WHY DON'T YOU JUST CALL HIM?

BEEP BEEP

A BOY WHO SMELLED LIKE LEMONS?

WHAT?

THE BOY WHO BOUGHT AN ADULT TICKET BY MIS-TAKE!

HUH?

MAYBE IT WAS THAT ONE BOY...

HE WAS WEARING A CAP AND CARRYING A BACK-PACK.

I DON'T REMEM-BER ANYONE LIKE THAT.

HE YELLED AT ME TO CHANGE HIS TICKET. HE SEEMED TO BE IN A BIG HURRY.

OH YEAH!

*About $19.

...SO MAYBE *GUNMA.*

IT WAS IN THE DIREC-TION OF CHIBA...

HMM... IT WAS A 1,900 YEN* ADULT TICKET.

DO YOU KNOW WHICH TRAIN HE TOOK?

YEAH, LIKE HE WAS BEING FOLLOWED...

IN A HURRY?

THE BURIED TREASURE OF THE TOKUGAWA CLAN!

HUH?

WHAT?

MAYBE THE BOY I SAW THIS MORNING WAS MITCH.

YES. HE SEEMS TO HAVE GONE OFF SOMEWHERE THIS MORNING.

SO HE'S MISSING, HUH?

NOT ANOTHER TREASURE HUNT...

AND MITCH WENT TO LOOK FOR IT!

IT MUST BE BURIED AT A BEACH SOMEWHERE!!

HE LOOKED LIKE MITCH, SO I SAID HI... BUT HE IGNORED ME AND GOT ON THE BUS.

I SAW A BOY AT THE SAME BUS STOP. HE HAD HIS CAP PULLED DOWN OVER HIS FACE AND HE WAS CARRYING A BACKPACK. AND HE SMELLED FUNNY!

THE SCENT OF LEMON?

A KIND OF **LEMONY** SCENT!

YEAH.

HE SMELLED FUNNY?

MAYBE AROUND 6:30 IN THE MORNING?

I DON'T THINK HE'S COME BY TODAY.

MITCH FROM THE FIRST GRADE?

OH...

Flower Shop FUJIWARA

I SEE.

THIS SHOP OPENS AT SEVEN. BEFORE THAT I WAS AT THE EXERCISES LIKE YOU GUYS, SO I DON'T KNOW WHO WAS HERE.

A COUPLE OF MEN WERE SCOLDING HIM.

BUT LAST SUNDAY I SAW HIM AT THE BUS STOP ON MY WAY TO THE EXERCISES.

NO, MAYBE IT WAS TOYOTOMI AND TOKU-GAWA...

UESUGI AND TAKEDA...

I DON'T REMEMBER... SOME OLD JAPANESE LORDS.

WHO'S "THEM"?

YEAH! ABOUT HOW HE SHOULDN'T LOOK FOR *THEM*!

SCOLD-ING HIM?

WHAT KIND OF DATE IS *THAT*?

...EATING BAMBOO DUMPLINGS?

...ON THE BEACH...

...WITH A GIRL...

...MITCH...

NO WONDER MITCH SOUNDS SO FORMAL.

OUR 'RENTS ARE TEACHERS, SO THEY'RE **SUPER STRICT** ABOUT MAKING US TALK RIGHT!

YES, MOTHER! I SHALL BE LEAVING PROMPTLY!

ASAMI! HURRY OR YOU'LL BE LATE FOR YOUR PIANO LESSON!

I WANT TO KNOW HOW HIS DATE WENT!

GIMME A CALL ON MY CELL IF YOU FIND ANYTHING INTERESTING!

CARE-FREE, ISN'T SHE?

SHE DOESN'T SEEM WORRIED THAT HER LITTLE BROTHER'S MISSING.

CHAK

♪

NO KID-DING.

HE'S BEEN SKIPPING THE EXERCISES EVERY SUNDAY.

LOOK! HIS RADIO EXERCISE STAMP CARD!

A GIRL?

NO WAY!

MAYBE HE'S GOT A *SECRET GIRL-FRIEND!*

WHAT'S HE BEEN DOING ON SUNDAY?

YOU'RE RIGHT.

...THE THIRD GRADE GIRL WHO HELPS OUT HER FAMILY'S FLOWER SHOP EVERY SUNDAY TOLD HIM HE WAS COOL.

COME TO THINK OF IT, MITCH TOLD ME...

BUT...

IT'S A COOL FOREIGN BRAND I ORDERED IN THE MAIL!

HE ASKED ME TO LOAN HIM MY SUNTAN LOTION!

HUH? WHY THE SEA-SIDE?

MAYBE HE TOOK THAT GIRL ON A SEA-SIDE DATE!

OOOH...

...AND HIS WALLET IS GONE.

WHAT? HIS WAL-LET?

HE HASN'T LEFT A NOTE...

SHF SHF

THIS IS GETTING KINDA WEIRD.

HEY... DOES THAT MEAN...

HE TOOK HIS WALLET AND FOOD THAT KEEPS FOR A LONG TIME. IT'S LIKE HE WAS PLANNING A BIG TRIP.

HE RAN AWAY FROM HOME.

WHAT?

WELL, WHETHER OR NOT HE RAN AWAY FROM HOME, HE'S BEEN PLANNING SOMETHING FOR A WHILE NOW.

IT'S NO LAUGH-ING MATTER!

OH, COOL! SERIOUSLY? IT'S LIKE A TV DRAMA! ♡

CAMPING?

HE TOLD ME HE WAS GOING CAMPING AFTER EXERCISES TODAY...

THAT'S WEIRD.

MITCH DIDN'T GO TO THE EXERCISES?

HUH?

HE WAS PACKING A *TON* OF BAMBOO DUMPLINGS.

YEAH. I SAW HIM GETTING READY FOR IT LAST NIGHT!

WELL, NO...

BUT FROM THE LOOKS OF THINGS, *YOU'RE* NOT ON THE CAMPING TRIP.

THE LADY NEXT DOOR GAVE THEM TO US!

BAMBOO DUMPLINGS?

MAYBE HE LEFT A NOTE.

WANT TO TAKE A LOOK IN HIS ROOM?

BEATS ME. USUALLY HE STICKS TO YOU KIDS LIKE GLUE.

SOMEPLACE HE'D GO WITHOUT TELLING US!

DON'T YOU HAVE ANY IDEA WHERE HE WENT?

...ISN'T HE?

...MITCH IS ABSENT AGAIN...

RIGHT.

MITCH IS USUALLY SO PUNCTUAL. HE'S NOT *SLOPPY* LIKE GEORGE...

SLOPPY?

WEIRD.

I WONDER WHAT'S WRONG WITH HIM. HE KEEPS SKIPPING THESE MORNING EXERCISES.

HE PROBABLY JUST OVERSLEPT!

WHY DON'T WE DROP BY HIS HOUSE LATER?

THEY'RE NOT TALKING ABOUT LOOSE SOCKS, GEORGE!

I'M DRESSED OKAY, AREN'T I?

WHEW

MAYBE HE CAUGHT A SUMMER COLD...

AND IF YOU DON'T EXERCISE DAILY YOU'LL LIVE TO REGRET IT.

THAT'S RIGHT!

A SIGNATURE EVENT?

RADIO EXERCISES ARE A SIGNATURE EVENT OF THE SUMMER!*

HEY! PAY ATTENTION!

*During summer break, many Japanese elementary schools organize morning exercises. They're still called *rajio taiso*, "radio exercises," but nowadays the lessons are usually on CD.

I KNOW *ONE* ADULT WHO NEEDS IT...

ONE! TWO! THREE! FOUR!

...WHICH COULD LEAD TO CEREBRO-VASCULAR DISORDERS AND ISCHEMIC HEART DISEASES!

YOU COULD GROW UP WITH HIGH BLOOD PRESSURE, DIABETES OR HYPER-CHOLES-TEREMIA...

IT MEANS IT MAKES YOU FEEL LIKE SUMMER IS HERE!

SIGNA-TURE EVENT!

WHAT'S THAT MEAN? THE SIGNING EVENT OF SUMMER OR WHATEVER...

SPEAKING OF THINGS YOU DON'T SEE...

...AND ALL THAT'S LEFT NOW ARE FIREWORKS AND RADIO EXERCISES!

DOC AGASA WAS TALKING ABOUT IT THE OTHER DAY ON THE WAY BACK FROM THE FIREWORKS SHOW! HE SAID YOU DON'T SEE MUCH OF THAT STUFF IN THE CITY THESE DAYS...

FILE 8:
MISSING MITCH ①

...PLUS THE MAN HIDING IN THE ABANDONED BUILDING. AFTER FOUR YEARS, THE CASE WAS CLOSED.

THE POLICE ARRIVED AND ARRESTED THE HOST OF OUR HAUNTED HOUSE...

WHAT A BACK-HAND...

THOK

IT WAS A TYPICAL TALE OF HUMAN WEAKNESS... A FAR CRY FROM A GHOST STORY.

IT TURNED OUT THEY'D KILLED THE WOMAN BECAUSE SHE OWED THEM A HUGE SUM OF MONEY. THEY LOST THEIR TEMPER WHEN SHE TOLD THEM SHE WAS GOING TO FILE FOR BANKRUPTCY RATHER THAN PAY THEM BACK.

THE WHOLE THING WAS JUST A *TRICK?*

NO WAY!

AND SO...

...IF THAT'S HOW YOU FEEL...

BE-CAUSE... BE-CAUSE...

SERENA, WHY ARE YOU CRYING?

SNIFF

THEY DON'T EXIST!

YEAH! I'M NOT AFRAID OF GHOSTS ANY-MORE!

...FOR THE MURDERER WHO WAS SPOTTED FOUR YEARS AGO. THE MAN WITH THE SCAR ON HIS FACE!

THAT'S RIGHT. THAT ABANDONED BUILDING IS THE PERFECT HIDEOUT...

IF YOUR ACCOMPLICE WAS CAUGHT, HE'D FINGER YOU AND YOU'D GO TO JAIL TOO.

PEOPLE SAW THE LIGHTS IN THE BUILDING AND STARTED TO SUSPECT THAT SOMEBODY WAS LIVING THERE. YOU DECIDED TO CREATE THIS GHOST STORY TO SCARE AWAY ALL THE PEOPLE LIVING ON THE SECOND FLOOR, WHICH HAD A VIEW OF THE BUILDING!

BANCHO IS PROBABLY THE OTHER MURDERER. HE WAS LUCKY ENOUGH TO AVOID BEING SEEN.

...

YOU MUST'VE PLANNED TO MAKE YOUR ESCAPE ONCE THINGS HAD CALMED DOWN, BUT NOW IT'S TOO LATE.

YOU LIVE HERE BECAUSE HE CAN'T GO OUT IN PUBLIC, SO YOU HAVE TO BRING HIM FOOD AND SUPPLIES.

WEEOO

THE SIRENS OF THE *POLICE CARS* I CALLED!!

WEEOO

THE SOUNDS OF YOUR DOOM ...

WEEOO

CAN YOU HEAR THEM?

A SWARM OF MALE MOTHS, TO BE EXACT.

...MOTHS!

MALE MOTHS WERE ATTRACTED TO THE CHEMICAL AND SWARMED ON THE WINDOW, CREATING A FACE.

PHEROMONES FROM FEMALE MOTHS ARE OFTEN USED IN PESTICIDES. BANCHO SPRAYED ONE OF THOSE CHEMICALS ON THE WINDOW SCREEN IN THE SHAPE OF A FACE AND ADDED EYES AND A MOUTH MADE FROM BLACK PAPER.

I JUST DETACHED THE SCREEN FROM THE WINDOW ON THE SECOND FLOOR AND REATTACHED IT HERE.

THEN THIS IS...

I ALMOST FELL OUT THE WINDOW THE FIRST TIME THE FACE APPEARED. SOME OF THE CHEMICAL GOT ON MY SLEEVE WHEN I GRABBED THE WINDOW.

REMEMBER HOW MOTHS KEPT LANDING ON MY SLEEVE?

THAT'S WHY HE SLAMMED THE WINDOW OPEN AND SHUT... TO SCARE AWAY ANY REMAINING MOTHS.

BUT BANCHO WORRIED THAT SOMEBODY WOULD FIGURE OUT THE TRICK IF EVEN A SINGLE MOTH STAYED ON THE WINDOW.

CHAK

MOTHS ARE EVEN MORE STRONGLY ATTRACTED TO ULTRAVIOLET RADIATION, LIKE THAT EMITTED BY BLACK LIGHTS, THAN THEY ARE TO PHEROMONES.

BANCHO COULD MAKE THE FACE FADE AWAY ON COMMAND BECAUSE HE'D SET A TIMER TO TURN ON THE BLACK LIGHTS IN HIS ROOM.

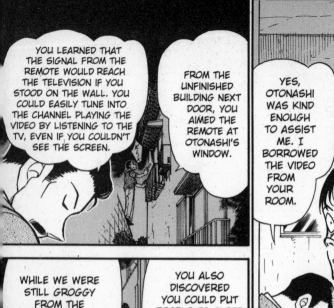

YOU LEARNED THAT THE SIGNAL FROM THE REMOTE WOULD REACH THE TELEVISION IF YOU STOOD ON THE WALL. YOU COULD EASILY TUNE INTO THE CHANNEL PLAYING THE VIDEO BY LISTENING TO THE TV, EVEN IF YOU COULDN'T SEE THE SCREEN.

FROM THE UNFINISHED BUILDING NEXT DOOR, YOU AIMED THE REMOTE AT OTONASHI'S WINDOW.

YES, OTONASHI WAS KIND ENOUGH TO ASSIST ME. I BORROWED THE VIDEO FROM YOUR ROOM.

THEN THE IMAGE THAT PLAYED ON MY TV...

WHILE WE WERE STILL GROGGY FROM THE CHLOROFORM, WE'D SPOT THE FACE IN THE WINDOW!

YOU ALSO DISCOVERED YOU COULD PUT PEOPLE TO SLEEP BY POURING *CHLOROFORM* INTO THE CONDENSER UNIT OF THE AIR CONDITIONER.

BUT IT'S NOT A FACE AT ALL.

LOOK, IT'S STARING AT US NOW!!

B...BUT *THAT'S* REAL, ISN'T IT?

I SEE...

IT... IT'S...

STEP UP AND HAVE A LOOK.

BANCHO PLAYED IT FROM THE VCR IN HIS ROOM!

THAT'S RIGHT. THAT'S THE GHOST MY DAUGHTER RACHEL SAW ON OTONASHI'S TELEVISION.

...YOU CAN SEND THE IMAGE TO THE TELE-VISIONS IN THE OTHER ROOMS!

IF YOU CONNECT THE OUTPUT TERMINAL OF THE VCR IN YOUR ROOM TO THE ANTENNA CABLE AND PLAY THE VIDEO...

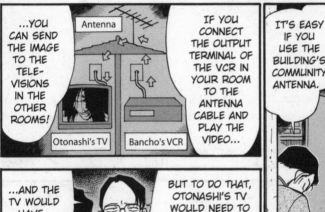

Antenna

Otonashi's TV

Bancho's VCR

IT'S EASY IF YOU USE THE BUILDING'S COMMUNITY ANTENNA.

BUT HOW'D HE DO THAT?

...AND THE TV WOULD HAVE TO BE TURNED ON.

BUT TO DO THAT, OTONASHI'S TV WOULD NEED TO BE TUNED TO THE SPECIFIC CHANNEL PLAYING THE TAPE...

YOU?

ONCE I KNEW THE TRICK, EVEN I COULD DO IT.

YOU CAN SET IT TO WORK WITH ANY MACHINE IF YOU KNOW THE MAKE AND MODEL. HE COULD CONTROL TVS AND VCRS ALL OVER THE BUILDING.

HE USED A *UNI-VERSAL REMOTE.*

HE SENT ME TO SNEAK INTO A ROOM WHILE EVERYBODY ELSE WAS IN THE FRONT HALL.

MR. MOORE ASKED ME TO HELP HIM.

WHERE'D YOU GET THAT, LITTLE BOY?

I SEE.

IF YOU MIX THIS INTO THE WATER IN THE TOILET BOWL, IT'LL CAUSE THE CHEMICAL REACTION. IT SMELLS BAD, BUT THIS BATHROOM IS SO DIRTY NO ONE WOULD SUSPECT *FOUL PLAY!*

IT WAS IN MR. BANCHO'S ROOM!

...AND A SCAAARY VIDEO.

...CHLOROFORM...

PHENOL-PHTHALEIN...

I FOUND A LOT OF OTHER STUFF THERE!

ISN'T THAT...

HEY...

UH-HUH! A WOMAN WHO LOOKS LIKE A GHOST KEEPS TELLING YOU TO GET OUT!

A SCARY VIDEO?

...IT TURNS RED LIKE MAGIC!

IF YOU ADD A DROP OF PHENOLPHTHALEIN AND ALCOHOL, WHICH ARE COLORLESS, TO AN EQUALLY COLORLESS BASE LIKE AMMONIUM...

I FIND IT HARD TO BELIEVE THAT EVEN *THESE* CREDULOUS NINNIES WOULD MISTAKE IT FOR *BLOOD*.

BUT THAT OLD EXPERIMENT JUST PRODUCES A PINKISHRED LIQUID.

...THE WATER WOULD TURN RED WHEN THE TWO MIXED TOGETHER DURING FLUSHING!

IN OTHER WORDS, IF THE TOILET TANK CONTAINED THE PHENOLPHTHALEIN MIXTURE AND THE WATER IN THE BOWL CONTAINED AMMONIA...

Phenolphthalein

Ammonia

EVEN IF THAT'S THE CASE, YOU WOULDN'T GET A CHEMICAL REACTION FROM URINE!

TRUE... BUT IN THE DIM LIGHTING OF THE BATHROOM, IT'D LOOK DARKER.

TH... THAT'S ...

...THIS BOTTLE OF AMMONIA!

POP

THAT'S RIGHT. THAT'S WHY HE NEEDED ...

URINE *DOES* CONTAIN AMMONIA, BUT IT'S NEUTRAL OR ACIDIC... NEVER BASIC.

DETECTIVE? HEH... YOU SOUND LIKE A DETECTIVE. A TRICK?

ISN'T *THAT* WHAT YOU'RE TRYING TO SAY, MR. BANCHO?

YOU GOT IT.

I KNOW YOU! YOU'RE *SLEEPING MOORE*, AREN'T YOU?

FIRST, THE WATER IN THE TOILET TURNING BLOOD RED.

...BEHIND THE STRANGE PHENOMENA IN THIS APARTMENT.

NOW LET'S START UNRAVELING THE SECRETS...

YOU ALL PROBABLY DID IT AS A SCIENCE EXPERIMENT IN GRADE SCHOOL.

AMMONIA AND ALCOHOL?

...AND I ALSO DETECTED A SLIGHT ODOR OF *ALCOHOL* IN THE WATER TANK.

WHENEVER IT HAPPENED, THE BATHROOM HAD A STRONG SMELL OF *AMMONIA*...

LOOK! THE TOILET REALLY *IS* CURSED!

HUH?

I THOUGHT YOU WERE GOING HOME!

WHAT? THE KID?

WE'VE GOT A PROBLEM!

IT STINKS REALLY BAD AND THE WATER WON'T FLUSH!

HMPH.

...BUT IT SHOULD FLUSH...

CHK

I KNOW IT STINKS...

...TURNED RED...

FWOOSH

TH... THE WATER...

FILE 7: THE MYSTERY OF THE HAUNTED HOUSE ③

OTONASHI DOESN'T MIND! HE HAS A WINDOW FACING THE STREET!

SEE FOR YOURSELF! THAT USELESS EDIFICE BLOCKS MOST OF THE SUNLIGHT TO MY ROOM!

SO I SEE...

SHOOF

CHAK

I THOUGHT HE ONLY BELIEVED IN *SCIENCE*...

THE RENT IS CHEAP... AND MY GRANDMOTHER TOLD ME THIS PLACE HAD GOOD FENG SHUI.

THEN WHY DON'T YOU MOVE?

...AND THE STRANGE IMAGE RACHEL SAW ON THE TV BOTH HAVE RATIONAL EXPLANATIONS.

THE WATER IN THE TOILET TURNING RED...

I STILL DON'T GET IT.

HUH?

GO RIGHT AHEAD.

'SCUSE ME. MIND IF I SMOKE?

SLAM

THAT WASN'T A *REFLECTION* IN THE WINDOWPANE. IT WAS... IT WAS...

BUT I'M NOT SO SURE ABOUT THE WILL O' THE WISP AND THE FACE IN THE WINDOW.

THIS WINDOW IS BENEATH THE WINDOW WHERE THE GHOSTLY FACE APPEARED.

CHAK

...BUT ONLY THROUGH THIS WINDOW.

YEAH, I DID...

BY THE WAY, IS IT TRUE YOU SAW THE WILL O' THE WISP TOO?

EEK!

LOOK, A COUPLE OF 'EM HAVE ALREADY GOTTEN IN...

FOR THE GIRL'S SAKE.

HEY, KID, I'D CLOSE THAT FAST IF I WERE YOU.

HUH?

HE'S ONE HARD-HEADED GRAD STUDENT...

IF YOU DON'T BELIEVE IN GHOSTS, YOU'LL GET ALONG WITH BOTAN IN ROOM 1!

WHY?

...IS THAT ABANDONED, HALF-COMPLETED BUILDING NEXT DOOR.

MY ONLY GRIPE...

I ONLY BELIEVE IN THINGS THAT CAN BE EXPLAINED SCIENTIFIC-ALLY.

TAK TAK

I HAVEN'T SEEN ANY OF THAT NON-SENSE.

YOU AIN'T SEEN NOTHIN' YET.

ALL THESE MODELS OF GHOSTS AND MONSTERS ...

HE WASN'T KIDDING.

WHOA ...

EEP!

IF YOU TURN OFF THE LIGHTS...

KLIK

THEY'RE ALL GLOWING IN DIFFERENT COLORS!!

TH... THE MODELS ...

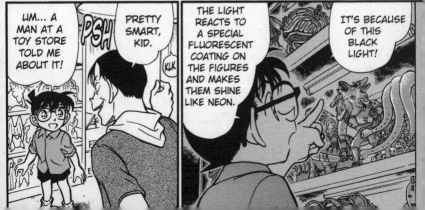

UM... A MAN AT A TOY STORE TOLD ME ABOUT IT!

PSH

KLIK

PRETTY SMART, KID.

THE LIGHT REACTS TO A SPECIAL FLUORESCENT COATING ON THE FIGURES AND MAKES THEM SHINE LIKE NEON.

IT'S BECAUSE OF THIS BLACK LIGHT!

DEAD HORROR

I USED TO SEE IT WHEN I DROPPED BY MY CLASSMATE'S OLD PLACE.

CLASSMATE?

YEAH, I'VE SEEN IT.

RED AND BLUE LIGHTS.

IN THE END HE MOVED OUT.

BUT AFTER THE GHOST STARTED APPEARING HE GOT SO SCARED HE COULDN'T SLEEP.

HE LIVED IN ROOM 6, THE ROOM RIGHT ABOVE MINE.

OH!

I SEE...

HEE HEE

I COULDN'T FALL ASLEEP EITHER... BECAUSE I WAS TOO *EXCITED*!

OH, I'M *NOTHING* COMPARED TO BANCHO IN ROOM 4.

I'D GET *NIGHTMARES* LIVING IN HERE.

YOU'VE GOT ONE HECK OF A PLACE. STUFFED TO THE GILLS WITH HORROR MAGAZINES, VIDEOS, POSTERS...

THAT'S RIGHT. I WAS SPLICING SOME FILM TOGETHER JUST NOW.

IS THAT AN 8MM FILM PROJECTOR?

CHK

...AND THIS WINDOW FACES THE BUILDING THAT'S UNDER CONSTRUCTION.

THE BUILDING IS SURROUNDED BY A HIGH WALL...

THAT'S THE AIR CONDITIONER.

SHOOF

OH... I WAS WONDERING WHERE IN THAT BUILDING MR. OTONASHI SAW THE WILL O' THE WISP.

WHY'D YOU OPEN THE WINDOW? YOU'LL LET THE MOTHS IN!

AT OTHER TIMES IT WAS *PALE BLUE.*

A SPECK OF *RED LIGHT* FLITTING SADLY ABOUT.

AROUND THE CENTRAL SECTION THERE.

THEY TOLD ME THEY'D SEEN IT BEFORE TOO.

IF YOU DON'T BELIEVE ME, ASK YOTSUYA IN ROOM 2 AND BANCHO IN ROOM 4.

ARE YOU TELLING ME I IMAGINED THAT *WOMAN* TOO?

THE CREEPY VIBE IN THIS BUILDING MADE US IMAGINE THINGS THAT WEREN'T THERE!

THE WATER JUST TURNED RED FROM RUST!

LOOK, THE FACE IN THE WINDOW WAS JUST SOMEONE'S REFLECTION!

BUT...

UNLESS THERE WAS *A HORROR MOVIE* PLAYING ON TV TONIGHT...

YOU DREAMED IT!

A WOMAN COVERED IN BURNS SAYING, "GET OUT"!

I REALLY SAW HER IN THE TV!

MY EARS ARE BURNING!

I DON'T THINK SO!

OR MAYBE THE OLD MAN PLAYED A WEIRD *VIDEO* TO MAKE US BELIEVE IN THE GHOST STORY...

MAYBE IT'S A CURSE!

CHK

THE *REAL* MYSTERY IS WHY WE ALL FELL ASLEEP AT THE SAME TIME...

THERE'S NO VIDEO IN THE VCR!

HUH?

BUT NOW THAT I THINK ABOUT IT, MAYBE IT WAS JUST RUST FROM THESE OLD PIPES.

IT SURE WASN'T *YELLOW*, KID.

DID THE WATER IN THIS TOILET *REALLY* TURN BLOOD RED?

WHAT ARE YOU DOING?

SNF SNF

...

STRANGE... LAST TIME I WAS IN HERE, THERE WAS A *STENCH*. NOW IT SMELLS FINE.

SMELLS LIKE ALCO-HOL...

HUH?

I GUESS YOU'RE RIGHT.

YOU LEFT THE DOOR OPEN. MAYBE THE ROOM JUST NEEDED TO BE VENTILATED.

GRR

THEY'LL ALL WANNA HEAR THE GHOST STORY THAT EVEN SCARED MR. MOORE!

BUT I WANNA INVESTIGATE EVERYTHING SO I CAN TELL THE OTHER KIDS AT SCHOOL!

HEY! DON'T MESS AROUND IN THERE!

IT'S JUST A BUG! GET A GRIP!!

SHEESH!!

SLAM

...AND SINCE IT'S NEARBY THEY FLY IN HERE A LOT.

THEY SAY EVER SINCE THE MURDER, THERE'VE BEEN *SWARMS* OF THEM IN THE PARK...

THAT "GHOSTLY" FACE WAS PROBABLY JUST SOMEONE'S *REFLECTION* DISTORTED IN AN ODD WAY.

WELL, IT WAS A SILLY THING TO SCREAM OVER.

YOU THINK SO? I THOUGHT IT WAS QUITE A *SCREAM*.

WELL, *THAT* RUINED THE GHOSTLY ATMOSPHERE.

ARE YOU CRAZY? THAT WAS THE REAL DEAL!

THAT'S RIGHT!

YOU TOO, CONAN. HURRY UP AND...

LET'S GO HOME!

WHAT'D I TELL YOU? IT WAS DUMB TO STICK AROUND HERE!

...IN MY WINDOW BEFORE.

I'VE SEEN THAT GHOST'S MISERABLE FACE...

YAWN

HUH?

...AND THE BODY'S TEETH MATCHED HER DENTAL RECORDS.

THE POLICE FOUND THE REMAINS OF HER DRIVER'S LICENSE...

RUI TABU-CHI?

WHAT YOU JUST SAW IS THE APPARITION OF RUI TABUCHI, WHO *BURNED TO DEATH* FOUR YEARS AGO.

I'M NOT SURPRISED IT TURNED TO ASH.

TWO MEN?

UNTIL THE TWO MEN WHO KILLED HER ARE ARRESTED, HER SPIRIT WILL NEVER REST IN PEACE.

CHK

LOOK OUT THE WINDOW AT THAT UTILITY POLE.

...AND SAW TWO MEN LOOKING DOWN AT THE BURNING BODY.

YES. SOMEONE HAPPENED TO PASS BY THE PARK...

SLAM

SOMEBODY SAW THEM?

SHOOF

...WHO WAS KILLED IN THE PARK!!

WHAT?

IT'S NOT THERE!

HEY!

SOME PUNK JUST CLIMBED UP TO THE WINDOW TO PLAY A PRANK ON US!

GHOST? WHAT A JOKE!!

NOOO!!

THE GHOST COULD BE ANYWHERE... EVEN IN *THIS VERY ROOM*...

WHAT DID YOU EXPECT?

HUH?

WATCH IT! THAT WINDOW'S...

MOVE ASIDE! I'LL CHECK IT OUT!

WHEN DID WE FALL ASLEEP?

WHOA, LOOK AT THE TIME!!

NO! I REALLY SAW HER!

ARE YOU SURE YOU DIDN'T JUST *DREAM* IT?

POK

O... OKAY...

WAKE UP THE OLD MAN AND TELL HIM WE'RE GOING HOME!

CHK

I'M GONNA GO TAKE A LEAK.

IT'S DARK, IT STINKS AND IT'S FULL OF DEAD BUGS!!

UGH! WHAT THE HECK?

WHAT A WASTE OF TIME...

CHK

HMPH... GHOSTS, MY FOOT.

HUH?

HOLD ON A SEC! I'M ALMOST...

DAD! COME HERE! THE OLD MAN WON'T WAKE UP!!

I SHOULD'VE LISTENED TO RACHEL AND GONE HOME RIGHT AWAY.

FLUUSH

KLNK

PSSSS

FZZT

GET
OUT
...

GET
OUT
...

GET
OUT
...

WHAT?

...BUT THEN *STRANGE THINGS* STARTED TO HAPPEN. WATER TURNED TO BLOOD, A GHOSTLY FIGURE APPEARED OUTSIDE OUR WINDOWS, AND WE SOMETIMES FELT FAINT AND SAW HORRIFIC VISIONS.

NONE OF THE RESIDENTS BELIEVED ME AT FIRST...

IT ALL STARTED WHEN I SAW AN EERIE LIGHT FLYING AROUND INSIDE THAT BUILDING NEXT DOOR.

AND I'VE GOT NO INTENTION OF LEAVING A PLACE WHERE I'VE LIVED FOR YEARS.

HA HA HA... I'M AN OLD MAN. I DON'T HAVE MUCH LONGER TO LIVE. GHOSTS DON'T SCARE ME!

SO WHY DIDN'T YOU LEAVE?

HMM ...

PEOPLE FROM TV STATIONS AND MAGAZINES CAME TO INTERVIEW US ABOUT IT.

NO, WE SHOULD GO NOW!

I'M SURE THE GHOST WON'T APPEAR UNTIL IT GETS DARK OUT.

WELL, MAKE YOUR-SELVES AT HOME.

OKAY, BUT ONLY UNTIL SEVEN O'CLOCK!

DAD!

IT SOUNDS FUN!

COME ON! THERE'S STILL TIME!

I HAVE A RESEARCH PAPER I HAVE TO FINISH BY TOMORROW.

I DON'T CARE IF YOU AMUSE YOURSELVES WITH SILLY GHOST STORIES, BUT PLEASE DON'T MAKE A RACKET.

THE FIRST-FLOOR RESTROOM WAS OCCUPIED, SO I WAS USING THE ONE ON THE SECOND FLOOR.

YOU'RE IN ROOM 1. WHAT WERE YOU DOING UP-STAIRS?

MR. BOTAN. HE GOES TO GRAD SCHOOL.

HE'S THE ONLY ONE HERE WHO'S NEVER SEEN THE GHOST.

WHO'S HE?

I'M IN ROOM 5 ON THE SECOND FLOOR.

CHAK

BUT THEN AGAIN, MOST PEOPLE WHO SAW THE GHOST MOVED OUT. IT'S JUST MR. BANCHO, MR. YOTSUYA AND ME.

SO THERE USED TO BE EIGHT PEOPLE IN THE BUILDING, BUT HALF OF THEM LEFT AFTER THIS *GHOST* STARTED TO APPEAR.

YEAH, THAT'S RIGHT.

HMM...

I HAVEN'T SEEN ONE AROUND LATELY.

IT'D LIVEN THE PLACE UP.

IWAHISA YOTSUYA (22)

MR. YOTSUYA IN ROOM 2. HE'S A HUGE FAN OF SCI-FI MOVIES, AND HIS ROOM'S PACKED WITH OLD VIDEOTAPES.

SLAM

AND THAT IS...?

CHAK

I HOPE IT COMES OUT...

...BUT HE'S NEVER SHOWN IT TO ME.

HE AND HIS COLLEGE FRIENDS MADE AN 8 MILLIMETER HORROR MOVIE BASED ON THE STORY OF THIS BUILDING...

IT'S SO JE-JUNE...

A JUVENILE FILM BASED ON CHILDISH SUPERSTITION. WHAT'S THE POINT?

TSUYUHIKO BOTAN (27)

DON'T WASTE YOUR TIME.

HA... WHAT A SIGHT.

YOU KNOW WHAT THEY SAY, DON'T YOU? GHOSTS ARE DRAWN TO PLACES...

EVENT-FUL?

THIS'LL BE AN EVENT-FUL NIGHT.

I THOUGHT OUR 15 MINUTES WERE UP, BUT IT LOOKS LIKE *SOMEBODY'S* STILL INTERESTED IN THAT GHOST.

...WHERE PEOPLE GATHER!!

KIKUJI BANCHO (34)

THAT'D BE GREAT!

WHAT'LL WE DO IF A GHOST REALLY APPEARS?

FLUSH

CHAK

C'MON, LET'S GO HOME!

HE WORKS IN A MODEL SHOP. HIS ROOM'S FULL OF SPOOKY-LOOKING FIGURINES.

MR. BANCHO. HE LIVES IN ROOM 4.

CHK

WHO WAS THAT?

WELL, WE CAN TALK MORE INSIDE.

...

CHAK

IT WAS BUILT OVER A *GRAVE-YARD.*

AND YOU SEE THIS HALF-FINISHED BUILDING? THE OWNER *HANGED* HIMSELF HERE WHEN THE ECONOMIC BUBBLE BURST, SO THE CONSTRUCTION WAS NEVER COMPLETED.

HE'S SETTING THE STAGE FOR A *GHOST STORY.*

I GET IT.

H-HEY, DAD...

L-LET'S GO...

AND CONAN WON'T GO WITH ME. HE'S TOO EXCITED ABOUT THE GH-GHOST...

GO HOME ALONE? I'M TOO SCARED!

YOU CAN HAIL A CAB AND GO HOME IF YOU WANT.

I D-DON'T THINK WE'LL GET ANYTHING OUT OF THIS...

I WAS KINDA LOOKING FORWARD TO SEEING THE HAUNTED HOUSE...

HUH...

LOOKS LIKE A PEACEFUL NEIGHBORHOOD TO ME.

THERE'S A LITTLE PARK ACROSS THE STREET.

SAD BUT TRUE...

...BUT IT'S JUST A *DUMP.*

SHE *BURNED* TO DEATH?

IT WAS COMPLETELY CHARRED.

...WHERE THEY FOUND THE WOMAN'S BODY.

THIS IS THE PARK...

WHAT?

I'VE MADE UP MY MIND! YOU'RE GOING TO BE MY DOCTOR FOR *LIFE!*

HMPH! DON'T HASSLE ME, BOY!

MR. OTONASHI! I THOUGHT I TOLD YOU NOT TO COME HERE ANYMORE!

THEY APPEAR IN MY APARTMENT TO DO MISCHIEF EVERY NOW AND THEN.

IT'S JUST THAT NARROW-MINDED PEOPLE DON'T SEE THEM.

WHAT?

...BUT HE WON'T RELOCATE TO THE HOSPITAL I RECOMMENDED.

HE USED TO BE A PATIENT OF MINE...

WHO'S THE GEEZER?

HOICHI OTONASHI (68)

WANT TO COME DOWN AND HAVE A LOOK?

OF COURSE!

IS THERE A GHOST IN YOUR APARTMENT?

IS THAT TRUE?

...SHE'S UNABLE TO REST IN PEACE.

IT'S THE WANDERING SPIRIT OF A YOUNG WOMAN WITH A GRUDGE SO STRONG...

THEY WENT OFF TO AOMORI AHEAD OF ME.

HEY, WHERE ARE YOUR GRANDMA AND THE MAID?

HEALTHY ENOUGH TO SCARE OFF A GHOST!

COME TO THINK OF IT, DR. ARAIDE OVERHEARD MY DEDUCTION. HE KNOWS THE *TRUTH* ABOUT THAT CASE.

AND I HAVE TO TESTIFY IN COURT ON MY FATHER'S MURDER, THAT SAD CASE MR. MOORE SOLVED FOR US...

YES, BUT I ASKED THE HOSPITAL IN AOMORI TO WAIT FOR ME UNTIL I CAN REASSIGN ALL MY PATIENTS TO OTHER CLINICS.

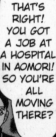

THAT'S RIGHT! YOU GOT A JOB AT A HOSPITAL IN AOMORI! SO YOU'RE ALL MOVING THERE?

WHY WOULD I?

YOU DON'T MIND LIVING IN THAT BIG OLD HOUSE ALL BY YOURSELF?

YES THEY DO.

THAT AGAIN!

THIS IS THE MODERN WORLD! GHOSTS DON'T EXIST HERE!

IT... IT'S JUST THE KIND OF HOUSE THAT COULD BE *HAUNTED* ...

AFTER DEALING WITH TWO MURDERS IN ONE DAY, I DIDN'T WANT TO REMIND YOU.

AH... RIGHT... DON'T WORRY, I'VE GOT IT!

SHOOT... WHERE DID I PUT THAT THING?

TWO MURDERS?

HUH?

BY THE WAY, WHATEVER HAPPENED TO SHARON'S HANDKERCHIEF?

YOU WENT INTO THE BUILDING TO GET IT FOR ME, RIGHT?

WOULD A GUY PLANNING TO KILL HIMSELF DO THAT?

BUT THE BLOOD ON THE FLOOR AND THE FINGERPRINTS ON THE DOORKNOBS AND RAILINGS HAD ALL BEEN WIPED CLEAN.

I JUST CHECKED UP ON THE DETAILS ONLINE.

THAT SERIAL KILLER COMMITTED SUICIDE, DIDN'T HE?

...BY SOMEBODY WHO GOT THERE **BEFORE** THE POLICE.

I THINK HE WAS GETTING READY TO MAKE A RUN FOR IT AND HAD JUST CLEANED UP HIS BLOOD AND PRINTS WHEN HE WAS KILLED...

YEAH... THAT'S WHAT THE POLICE SAID.

IT'S ME!!

CHAK

I HEAR SOMEBODY AT THE DOOR.

AT THE DOOR?

HEY, HANG ON.

CAPTAIN RADISH WAS LOOKING INTO IT, BUT I GUESS HE NEVER FOUND ANY LEADS.

WERE YOU WORRIED ABOUT ME, JIMMY?

YEAH.

NO WONDER YOU DIDN'T ANSWER ANY OF THE MESSAGES I LEFT ON YOUR CELL.

DOWN WITH A FEVER, HUH?

THAT'S NONE OF YOUR BUSINESS!

WORRIED THAT YOU HADN'T PAID YOUR PHONE BILL!

AND THAT FEVER JOGGED MY MEMORY OF NEW YORK!

I'M GOING FOR A CHECKUP AT DR. ARAIDE'S CLINIC, BUT I'M FINE!

YOU BET!

SO ARE YOU FEELING BETTER?

IT WASN'T *ALL* BAD...

NO, IT'S OKAY!

I HOPE IT DIDN'T UPSET YOU TOO MUCH...

AH... THAT UGLY CASE, HUH?

I WENT THROUGH SO MUCH AND MET SO MANY PEOPLE...

HOW COULD I HAVE FORGOTTEN SOMETHING SO IMPORTANT? I GUESS ALL THE BAD MEMORIES STOPPED ME FROM REMEMBERING THE GOOD PARTS.

THE DAY I KNEW I HAD FEELINGS FOR... WELL...

WHO WAS HE?

THAT'S RIGHT! THE MAN IN THE BLACK CAP WAS THERE TOO!

FBI?

WHAT'S THAT SUP-POSED TO MEAN?

THOSE WORDS ARE *MINE!* I DON'T WANT TO HEAR THEM COMING OUT OF YOU!

FWUMP

HUH?

FORGET YOU HEARD THAT!

NO !!

SLEEP TIGHT, RACHEL!

ER... ANYWAY... I'LL BE TAKING YOU HOME TOMORROW. TRY TO GET A GOOD NIGHT'S SLEEP!

CLICK

THAT WAS THE DAY.

THE DAY I KNEW.

I'D FOR-GOTTEN ALL ABOUT THAT DAY.

I SEE.

WHAT?

YOU NEED TO CUT DOWN ON THE EXTRA-CURRICULAR ACTIVITIES!

YOU WERE SUFFERING FROM EXHAUS-TION.

RACHEL! YOU'RE UP!

ALL RIGHT! HER FEVER'S GONE DOWN, JUST LIKE THE DOCTOR SAID!

HUH?

HUH?

HE BROUGHT YOU HERE AT FULL SPEED IN THE PATROL CAR!

BE SURE TO THANK INSPECTOR YOKOMIZO'S BROTHER!

ACK!

SOMETHING ABOUT SAVING PEOPLE... AND LOGICAL REASONS...

OH?

BY THE WAY, YOU WERE MUTTERING FUNNY STUFF DURING YOUR FEVER.

...SHE SEEMS TO HAVE FORGOTTEN EVERYTHING THAT HAPPENED.

FUNNY THING IS...

SHE WAS IN BED LAST NIGHT WITH A FEVER, BUT IT LOOKS LIKE A GOOD NIGHT'S SLEEP FIXED HER UP.

YES, RACHEL'S DOING FINE!

BY THE WAY, COULD YOU PASS ON A MESSAGE TO RACHEL?

BUT I NEVER IMAGINED SHE WAS PLOTTING *MURDER.*

WELL... I'VE ALWAYS HAD A SIXTH SENSE.

HEY, SHARON... YOU KNEW ABOUT IT, DIDN'T YOU? YOU HAD A HUNCH THAT ROSE WAS GOING TO DO SOMETHING...

...I SEEM TO HAVE A GUARDIAN ANGEL TOO.

TELL HER...

I SAID I'M FINE!

LET ME CHECK YOUR FOREHEAD...

I'M FINE, I'M FINE!

HEY, DO YOU STILL HAVE A FEVER?

...

MORE OR LESS...

OH? RUN INTO SOME GOOD LUCK?

...AND PUT YOU BEHIND BARS FOR GOOD. BE READY!

I'M GOING TO TALLY UP ALL YOUR SINS...

BUT NEXT TIME I SEE YOU, DON'T EXPECT ANY MERCY.

SHAAA

BUT BY THE TIME THEY REACHED THE SCENE, THE GUY HAD ALREADY SHOT HIMSELF.

JIMMY'S THE ONE WHO CALLED THE POLICE!

THEY FOUND THAT SERIAL KILLER!

DID YOU SEE THE NEWS?

I'M SO...

WHY DIDN'T I REALIZE THAT?

HE'S RIGHT...

RIGHT...

HUH? HEY, RACHEL!

DON'T DO IT.

SHK

...SO I'LL HAVE TO LET YOU GO FOR NOW.

I'M IN NO CONDITION TO APPREHEND YOU MYSELF...

THAT GUN DOESN'T HAVE A SILENCER. THE MINUTE YOU FIRE, THE COPS WILL BE ON YOU.

YOU'RE WOUNDED. YOU'RE ON THE RUN.

WELL, PASS ON A MESSAGE TO THAT FRIEND OF YOURS...

HE'S A FRESHMAN AT MY HIGH SCHOOL, SAME AS ME...

NO... MY FRIEND...

I'M WAITING FOR MY FRIEND HERE!

TURN RIGHT AT THAT CORNER UP AHEAD AND YOU'LL HIT A MAJOR STREET. YOU CAN CATCH A TAXI THERE.

GET OUT OF THIS PART OF TOWN!!

BEAT IT!!

THAT *SLASHER.*

I KNEW IT. HE'S AROUND HERE SOME-WHERE.

SHOULD WE LEAVE HER HERE?

HEY!

UM... JIMMY?

I'VE GOT TO TELL JIMMY.

DON'T WORRY... WE'VE GOT EVERY EXIT COVERED.

A JAPANESE GUY WITH LONG SILVER HAIR AND STUBBLE.

HUH?

SEE ANYBODY SUSPICIOUS AROUND HERE?

UM...

...YES!!

I'M ASKING YOU IF YOU'RE JAPANESE.

SKREE

N... NO, I HAVEN'T SEEN ANY- BODY...

NO, JUST A TOURIST. GUESS HE DIDN'T COME THIS WAY.

DID YOU FIND HIM, SIR?

CHAK

ANYWAY, THIS IS A DANGEROUS ALLEY.

GRP

...SO I DON'T THINK HE'D PASS UP PREY LIKE THIS GIRL.

THAT ANIMAL'S ALL HOPPED UP FROM TRADING GUNFIRE WITH US...

YOU'VE BEEN A BIG HELP...

GOD WOULD NEVER MAKE YOU GO THROUGH THIS.

IT'S MY FAULT...

IT'S...

BECAUSE I SAVED ROSE, HEATH DIED.

IT'S ALL MY FAULT.

DID SHE KNOW I'D SAVED A MURDERER?

...ROSE WAS GOING TO KILL SOMEBODY?

DID SHARON KNOW...

ZHK

SHARON GAVE IT TO ME!

IT'S NOT JUST *ANY* HANDKERCHIEF!

FORGET ABOUT IT! IT'S JUST A HANDKERCHIEF!

STRANGE... IT SHOULD BE HERE SOMEWHERE. MAYBE THE WIND BLEW IT ONTO A ROOF...

WHAT?

SEE? THERE IS NO GOD...

LOOK! THAT WHITE THING STUCK ON THE FIRE ESCAPE!

THERE IT IS!

HEY!

GO ON BACK TO THE TAXI!

I'LL GET IT FOR YOU!

...

THIS LOOKS LIKE AN ABANDONED BUILDING.

SHK

SHE NEVER DIDN'T SAY ANYTHING IMPORTANT.

WHAT DID SHE SAY? SHE WAS TALKING SO FAST, I COULDN'T FOLLOW HER ENGLISH.

HUH? ROSE?

YOU'RE NOT BUGGED BY WHAT ROSE SAID AT THE END, ARE YOU?

THE DRIVER'S GOING TO BE TICKED OFF IF YOU GET HIS SEAT ALL WET WITH RAIN.

AND I CAN'T SEE NEW YORK AT NIGHT WITH THE WINDOW CLOSED!

I'M FINE NOW!

NOW CLOSE THE WINDOW BEFORE YOU CATCH A COLD! YOU HAD A LITTLE FEVER TODAY, DIDN'T YOU?

BYU

HMPH...

DON'T WORRY! I'LL WIPE OFF THE SEAT WITH THIS HANDKERCHIEF WHEN WE GET OUT!

PLEASE!

SIR! PLEASE STOP THE CAR!

HYOOO

HEY...

SKREE

YEAH, YEAH!

HE'S A JAPANESE GUY WITH LONG HAIR...

OH, AND WATCH OUT FOR THAT STREET SLASHER!

SEE YOU LATER, JIMMY! I HAVE TO DROP BY THE POLICE FOR SOME QUESTIONING. GET A TAXI AND CHECK INTO THE HOTEL FOR US!

NO PROB.

EVERY-BODY TREATS ME LIKE A KID!

GEEZ... I'M IN HIGH SCHOOL, YOU KNOW.

VROOM

IT'S LIKE HOLMES SAID.

SHAAAA

OH WELL.

WHAT'S WRONG, RACHEL?

HUH?

...

"IF WE WENT ROUND THE MOON IT WOULD NOT MAKE A PENNYWORTH OF DIFFERENCE TO ME OR TO MY WORK"!

BUT
MMY...
WHEN
D YOU
SPECT
RE WAS
OOD
HER?

...SO THE POLICE WOULDN'T FIND ANY GUNPOWDER RESIDUE ON IT!

SHE PROBABLY WORE THE GLOVE INSIDE OUT WHILE SHE WAS ONSTAGE, THEN TURNED IT BACK AROUND AFTER SHOOTING HEATH...

HEATH'S BLOODY HAND-PRINTS!

I WONDERED WHY SHE DIDN'T JUST TAKE OFF HER GLOVES TO OPEN THE CAN. SHE MUST'VE BEEN HIDING SOMETHING UNDERNEATH!

IT WAS WHEN SHE HAD TROUBLE OPENING THAT CAN OF SODA IN THE DRESSING ROOM!

BUT THE PHOTO ON ROSE'S MIRROR WAS...

PICTURES OF THEM TOGETHER WITH HEATH.

YOU SAW THEM ON LILA'S AND AKANE'S MIRRORS, RIGHT?

HUH?

THAT'S WHEN I FIGURED OUT HER MOTIVE FOR KILLING HEATH TOO.

...THE ANGEL.

DON'T YOU GET IT? THEY COULD HIDE THE TRAP DOOR FROM THE REST OF THE CAST BY REVOLVING THE STAGE, BUT THEY NEEDED ROSE TO REACH UNDER THE MIRROR AND CLOSE THE GRATE AFTER HEATH ROSE INTO THE AIR!

BUT WHY DID THEY TELL ROSE?

THEY ONLY TOLD HEATH AND ROSE!

THAT'S WHY THEY DECIDED TO USE THE UNDERSTAGE TO HIDE HEATH FROM VIEW!

BEFORE SHE SHOT HEATH, SHE POINTED THE LASER SIGHT AT THE TERRACE TO DISTRACT THE AUDIENCE.

ROSE PROBABLY HID IT IN HER DRESS AND PULLED IT OUT AFTER ENOUGH SMOKE HAD RISEN TO CONCEAL HER.

WHAT ABOUT THE GUN?

SHE STUCK IT IN THE FRILLS OF HIS COSTUME SO IT WOULD FALL AS HE ROSE, MAKING IT LOOK LIKE IT HAD BEEN THROWN FROM THE BALCONY.

ROSE PUT THE HOT GUN THERE RIGHT AFTER FIRING.

REMEMBER THAT BURN MARK ON HIS CHEST?

YOU BET SHE COULD! SHE USED HEATH'S BODY TO DO IT!

BUT THAT GUN FELL TO THE STAGE FROM ABOVE! SHE COULDN'T HAVE THROWN IT THAT HIGH INTO THE AIR IF SHE WAS LYING DOWN!

THEY SHOULD STILL BE THERE... ON HER RIGHT HAND AND GLOVE...

THE SMEARED BLOODSTAIN ON HEATH'S HAND PROVES THAT HE GRABBED HER AS HE ROSE.

WHAT?

BUT I BET SHE NEVER EXPECTED HEATH TO *GRAB HER ARM* WITH HIS BLOODY HAND.

ROSE...
YOU'RE IT.

I KNOW. THERE WAS A REASON FOR THAT.

NOBODY TOLD US WE'D BE USING THAT OLD TRAP DOOR!

ROSE...

NO... IT CAN'T BE HER...

...THAT YOUR LUCKY CHARM HAD BEEN BROKEN.

THE STAGE-HANDS DIDN'T WANT TO LET YOU ACTORS KNOW...

THEY KEPT IT SECRET, KNOWING HOW SUPERSTITIOUS THE CAST WAS ABOUT THE MIRROR. BUT ONCE THE MIRROR WAS SHORTENED, HEATH WOULDN'T FIT BEHIND IT.

THE MIRROR USED TO BE TALLER. EARLIER TODAY, THE STAGEHANDS FOUND A CRACK AT THE TOP, PROBABLY MADE BY ROSE. THEY FIXED IT BY CUTTING OFF THE TOP OF THE MIRROR AND SHORTENING THE FRAME.

...BLOOD THAT SPILLED FROM HIS BODY...

SOME MORE FEATHERS FROM HEATH'S WINGS...

I BET THEY'LL FIND SOME INTERESTING THINGS IN THERE.

IT'S A TRAP DOOR, CAPTAIN!!

OKAY, CHECK IT OUT!

YUP. HEATH WAS SHOT WHILE HE WAS WAITING JUST INSIDE THE TRAP DOOR.

THE SHELL CASE? DOES THAT MEAN HE WAS SHOT FROM CLOSE RANGE?

...AND THE SHELL CASE FROM THE GUN!

BANG

THE MURDERER STUCK HER HAND UNDER THE MIRROR AND THROUGH THE IRON GRATE TO SHOOT HIM!

...WAS THE PERSON WHO WAS LYING ON THE FLOOR IN FRONT OF THE MIRROR.

THAT'S RIGHT... THE ONLY PERSON WHO COULD HAVE DONE IT...

THEN THE MURDERER IS...

...THE TRAP DOOR AND UNDER-STAGE!!

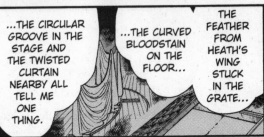

...THE CIRCULAR GROOVE IN THE STAGE AND THE TWISTED CURTAIN NEARBY ALL TELL ME ONE THING.

...THE CURVED BLOODSTAIN ON THE FLOOR...

THE FEATHER FROM HEATH'S WING STUCK IN THE GRATE...

BUT THERE WASN'T ANY TRAP DOOR BEHIND THE MIRROR. JUST THAT FUNNY GRATE IN THE FLOOR...

KREEE

THIS CIRCULAR SECTION OF THE STAGE MOVES AROUND...

SNAP

YOU DUMMY! WHAT DO YOU THINK WAS *UNDER* THE GRATE?

CHOK

...APPEAR BEFORE OUR VERY EYES!!

KREEE

...MAKING THE HIDDEN UNDER-STAGE...

...AND IBLIS WAS SITTING DOWN WHEN IT HAPPENED.

AKANE WAS KNEELING ON THE FLOOR, ROSE WAS LYING ON THE GROUND...

...THAT A WOMAN WHO WAS SHORTER THAN HEATH WAS ABLE TO SHOOT *DOWN* AT HIM.

IT'S HARD TO BE-LIEVE...

HUH?

RIGHT... AND TO TOP IT OFF, NO ONE COULD'VE SHOT HEATH WHILE HE WAS BEHIND THE MIRROR.

LILA WAS THE ONLY ONE STANDING UP... BUT YOU SAID YOURSELF THAT THE WHOLE AUDIENCE COULD SEE HER HANDS, SO SHE COULDN'T HAVE SHOT A GUN WITHOUT BEING NOTICED!

WHEN I HAD YOU HOLD A PROGRAM OVER YOUR HEAD TO APPROXIMATE THAT HEIGHT, YOU AND THE PROGRAM WERE *TALLER* THAN THE MIRROR.

DON'T YOU THINK IT'S FUNNY? HEATH WAS 6'3".

BUT THAT'S ONLY IF HEATH REALLY *WAS* STANDING BEHIND THE MIRROR!

WHAT?

IT'S A COMMON STAGE DEVICE THAT ALLOWS AN ACTOR TO APPEAR AND DISAPPEAR. WE USE THEM IN KABUKI SHOWS IN JAPAN...

THE MURDERER TOOK ADVANTAGE OF AN OLD THEATER TRICK.

AND THE WINGS HEATH WAS WEARING KEPT HIM FROM BENDING HIS KNEES. HE COULDN'T HAVE HIDDEN BEHIND THE MIRROR WITHOUT HIS HEAD POKING OVER THE TOP.

...IT WAS IMPOSSIBLE FOR **ANY** OF YOU TO HAVE SHOT HIM.

HMM... JUDGING FROM WHERE THE FOUR OF YOU WERE...

I CAN'T DENY IT...

THIS MEANS IT WAS SOMEBODY FROM THE OUTSIDE.

MAY WE CHANGE OUT OF OUR COSTUMES NOW?

WHAT?

FWASH

SURE... WE DIDN'T FIND ANY GUN-POWDER RESIDUE ON YOU.

BUT I LIKE TO CALL MYSELF...

SOME CALL ME THE LEGENDARY BEAUTY OF JAPANESE SHOW BIZ...

WHO TURNED OUT THE LIGHTS?

FWASH

...THE LADY DETECTIVE WITH THE HOT GREY MATTER...

...OTHERS THE WIFE OF THE WORLD'S GREATEST MYSTERY WRITER.

ME!

WHAT ARE YOU TALKING ABOUT? WE DON'T NEED IT FOR THIS SHOW...

YOU GUYS ARE THE ONES WHO WORKED THE STAGE DEVICE, RIGHT?

COME ON! I SAID "PLEASE," DIDN'T I?

I JUST NEED YOU TO MOVE IT A LITTLE!

GULP

AHA! SO YOU *ARE* THE ONES WHO WORK IT!

HOW ABOUT *ME*...

WE'RE NOT GOING TO TELL SOME STRANGE KID ABOUT IT!!

EITHER WAY, THAT'S THE PRIVATE BUSINESS OF THE COMPANY!!

WE WEREN'T SURE IF WE SHOULD GO TO THE COPS ABOUT IT...

OF COURSE, MA'AM!

WHOA!!

...THE NIGHT BARONESS?

...WITH A CIRCULAR GROOVE NEARBY...

IT'S STUCK IN THIS PLAIN IRON GRATE...

WHAT'S IT DOING HERE?

A FEATHER?

...BLOOD?

IS THIS...

CHOK

HEY...

THE MURDERER USED SOMETHING UNIQUE TO THE STAGE...

I'VE GOT IT!

SHE'S AS WILY AS THE GODDESS ERIS!

...TO SET UP THIS MURDER!

A CRACK...

HEY... JIMMY...

SUPER-STITIOUS ACTORS.

THAT'S FUNNY. SHARON TOLD ME THEY TAKE VERY GOOD CARE OF THIS MIRROR. IT'S BEEN A PART OF THE THEATER FOR GENERATIONS, AND IT'S KIND OF A GOOD-LUCK CHARM.

RIGHT ABOVE YOU. A LITTLE CRACK IN THE MIRROR.

HUH?

HUH?

HOW CAREFUL COULD THEY HAVE *BEEN*?

LOOK, IT'S BEEN TAKEN APART AND GLUED BACK TOGETH-ER!

?!

C'MON, LET'S GET BACK. YOUR MOM'S GOING TO KILL US...

MAYBE SOMEBODY GOT TANGLED UP IN IT DURING THE RUSH OUT.

THE CURTAIN'S KIND OF TWISTED.

DON'T HOLD BACK! TELL ME!!

YOU KNOW SOMETHING, DON'T YOU?

HEY, JIMMY!

HEY, RACHEL... HOW TALL ARE YOU?

160 CENTIMETERS!

THAT'S ABOUT 5'3".

WHO ARE THOSE KIDS?

DUNNO. THE CAPTAIN TOLD ME TO LEAVE THEM ALONE.

SORRY, BUT COULD YOU HOLD THIS OVER YOUR HEAD AND STAND IN FRONT OF THE MIRROR FOR ME?

WHAT?

THIS PROGRAM IS ABOUT 12 INCHES HIGH...

ONE FOOT...

HMM...

HUH?

HM...

UM... HOW IS THIS SUPPOSED TO HELP?

LILA HAD THE BEST CHANCE OF SHOOTING DOWNWARD, SINCE SHE WAS THE ONLY ONE STANDING...

AKANE WAS KNEELING DOWN IN PRAYER.

IBLIS HAD FALLEN TO THE FLOOR.

...BUT SHE WAS LYING ON THE FLOOR IN A FAKE FAINT.

ROSE WAS CLOSEST TO THE MIRROR AT THE TIME...

...BUT WHILE THE OTHERS' HANDS WERE HIDDEN IN THE SMOKE, HERS WERE CLEARLY VISIBLE. IT WOULD'VE BEEN OBVIOUS IF SHE'D PULLED A GUN.

...

DON'T *YOU* HAVE ANY IDEAS, JIMMY?

HMM ...

HE COULDN'T HAVE. THE WINGS WERE CONTROLLED BY A BRACE ON HIS LEGS WHICH KEPT HIM FROM BENDING HIS KNEES.

MAYBE HEATH WAS KNEELING BEHIND THE MIRROR.

HUH?

YES. HEATH AND I WERE IN LOVE.

HEY, WHAT YOU TOLD ME... IS IT TRUE, LILA?

BUT YOU KNEW WE WERE TOGETHER! HOW COULD YOU BETRAY ME LIKE THAT?

WE'D BEEN SEEING EACH OTHER FOR FIVE YEARS.

HM.

COULD YOU TWO CALM DOWN? SAVE IT FOR ANOTHER NIGHT...

POK

SKCH SKCH

THEN SOME-BODY *MADE* IT FALL!

THE STRING IS TIED TO THE ARMOR.

...AND A MARK ON THE FLOOR, LIKE IT WAS SLASHED WITH A BLADE.

A THIN NYLON STRING TIED TO A NAIL...

SHE KNEW EVERYONE WOULD PASS BY HERE DURING THE BACK-STAGE TOUR.

YEAH... SHE MUST'VE CUT THE STRING WITH A BLADE ATTACHED TO HER SHOE AS SHE WALKED BY.

ANY ONE OF THE FOUR GODDESSES COULD'VE DONE IT!!

ONLY SOMEBODY WHO WAS IN THE GROUP AT THAT TIME COULD'VE DROPPED THE ARMOR, AND ONLY SOMEBODY WHO WAS ONSTAGE WITH HEATH COULD'VE SHOT HIM WHILE POINTING A LASER AT THE BALCONY.

Dressing Room

OH...

ER... I HAVEN'T FIGURED THAT OUT YET.

THAT'S RIGHT! HOW, JIMMY?

BUT HEATH IS 6'3"! HOW COULD ANY OF THOSE WOMEN SHOOT *DOWN* AT HIM? BESIDES, HE WAS BEHIND THAT MIRROR!

AHA AHA

YOU THINK THE KILLER IS ONE OF THE FOUR ACTRESSES?

THAT'S CRAZY!

I FOUND A SHELL CASING ON THE BALCONY RIGHT AFTER THE MURDER... BUT THE METAL WAS *COOL.*

SOMEBODY PLANTED IT THERE AHEAD OF TIME.

BUT YOU SAW IT TOO, DIDN'T YOU? THE RED LIGHT FROM A LASER SIGHT FLASHING DOWN ONTO THE STAGE!

YEAH, THAT'S WHAT IT LOOKED LIKE...

...BUT WE COULDN'T REALLY TELL WHERE THE LASER WAS COMING FROM.

I BET THE MURDERER POINTED IT *UP* FROM THE STAGE... TO MAKE US THINK SOMEBODY WAS TRYING TO AIM FROM THE BALCONY.

PUTTING ON AN OBVIOUS DISGUISE TO BUY TICKETS... SENDING THAT CREEPY GIFT BACKSTAGE... IT WAS ALL A PLOT TO THROW US OFF TRACK.

For the Fairest

TAKE A LOOK AT THE FLOOR.

THIS IS WHERE THE SUIT OF ARMOR FELL.

AND HERE'S ANOTHER TRICK.

YOU COULD BE RIGHT.

OH... I SEE.

WHOOOA

JIMMY?

...I BET *JIMMY* COULD FIGURE IT OUT!

NO, HE WAS INVOLVED IN THE INVESTI- GATION FROM THE VERY START!

OH, I'M SURE AFTER THE CROOK WAS CAUGHT HE TOLD YOU HE'D KNOWN WHO IT WAS ALL ALONG. HE LOVES TO BRAG... ♡

BUT HE SOLVED A CASE WHILE WE WERE ON THE PLANE TO AMERICA!

COME ON! HE'S STILL A KID! HE'S NEVER INVESTIGATED A REAL MURDER BEFORE...

...JUST LIKE HOLMES OR POIROT.

YES. HE LINED UP ALL THE SUSPECTS AND TOLD THEM HOW IT HAPPENED WITH THAT SMUG LOOK OF HIS...

HE WAS?

HUH?

IS THAT SO, JIMMY?

HMM ...

LIKE WHAT?

THERE ARE A COUPLE OF FUNNY THINGS HERE...

I DON'T GET IT.

IT'S A RED HERRING...

WHAT?

THE THEATER WOULD REMEMBER A SUSPICIOUS PERSON WHO SPECIFICALLY ASKED FOR A BAD SEAT.

AND THERE'S BLOOD ON HIS RIGHT HAND.

YOU SEE THAT BURN MARK ON HIS CHEST?

I GUESS SO... FOR NOW.

SO HAS THIS ONE STUMPED EVEN THE NIGHT BARONESS?

THAT SUGGESTS HE TOUCHED SOMETHING *AFTER* THE BLOOD GOT ON HIS HAND, BUT THERE ARE NO BLOODSTAINS ON HIS COSTUME. AND WHAT ELSE COULD HE TOUCH WHILE HE WAS HANGING IN MIDAIR?

NO... THE BLOOD ON HIS HAND IS *SMEARED.*

MAYBE HE GRABBED HIS CHEST AFTER BEING SHOT.

HEY...

I'LL BE HEARING IT FROM THE PUBLIC, THE COMMISH *AND* MY WIFE...

ARGH... WHAT A SHAME. A CELEBRITY MURDERED, AND I DON'T HAVE A SINGLE LEAD.

NO! BOOKER'S LOCKED IN A HOTEL ROOM IN L.A., WORKING.

WHY NOT ASK BOOKER? I BET HE'D HAVE SOME IDEAS.

HMPH! *THIS* ONE'S REAL...

BOING

OUCH!

WHAT IS IT?

EXCUSE ME, CAPTAIN...

DOESN'T HE LOOK JUST LIKE BOOKER? AND JUST AS SPIRITED!

IS THIS LITTLE JIMMY, THE BOY YOU'RE ALWAYS BRAGGING ABOUT?

HM?

IT'S JUST LIKE YOU SAID, VIVIAN.

YEAH, YEAH...

STAY OUT OF THE WAY, JIMMY!

THOSE SEATS ARE CALLED THE GODS. THEY'RE HIGH AND ANGLED AWAY FROM THE STAGE, SO THE VIEW ISN'T TOO GOOD.

HEY, WHY ARE THOSE SEATS CHEAP? THEY LOOK SO FANCY!

THAT'S GOT TO BE THE KILLER!

BUT THE PERSON WAS DISGUISED IN A HAT AND SCARF. WE DON'T EVEN KNOW IF IT WAS A MAN OR A WOMAN.

A SUSPICIOUS-LOOKING PERSON BOUGHT A TICKET FOR ONE OF THOSE CHEAP SEATS ABOUT A MONTH AGO.

VIVIAN?

NIGHT BARONESS!!

...USING A LASER TO GUIDE THE SHOT.

IT'S A FANTASTIC SCENE WITH FIREWORKS AND SMOKE. AFTER THE IMAGE OF THE ANGEL APPEARS IN THE MIRROR, HEATH RISES FROM BEHIND IT IN HIS ANGEL COSTUME, MAKING IT LOOK LIKE HE'S FLYING OUT OF THE MIRROR.

IT HAPPENED DURING THE BIG FINALE, WHEN THE ANGEL APPEARS.

I JUST CAME TO WATCH THE SHOW.

I WAS EXPECTING A MUSICAL, NOT A MURDER MYSTERY.

WHAT ARE YOU DOING HERE?

RIGHT. AFTER THE GUN WAS THROWN ONSTAGE, THE AUDIENCE PANICKED, MAKING IT EASY FOR THE KILLER TO ESCAPE.

SO THE MURDERER SHOT HIM WHEN HE CAME OUT FROM BEHIND THE MIRROR...

HUH?

HE'S STANDING RIGHT NEXT TO YOU.

YOUR SON?

MY SON SAW IT TOO.

YES! THANKS TO ALL THE SMOKE ON THE STAGE, WE COULD CLEARLY SEE THE THIN RED LINE OF THE LASER POINTING FROM THAT SECTION.

BUT ARE YOU SURE THE VICTIM WAS SHOT FROM THE BALCONY SEATS?

YOU KNOW HIM, CAPTAIN?

I CAN'T BELIEVE IT! HEATH FLOCKHEART!!

GOOD LORD!!

MY WIFE'S A BIG FAN OF HIS.

WE'VE ASKED THE ACTORS TO WAIT IN THEIR DRESSING ROOMS, BUT MOST OF THE AUDIENCE HAS FLED.

SO WHAT'S THE SITUATION?

AH, YOU MEAN THESE...

WUP

WINGS?

THE BULLET WENT THROUGH HIS CHEST. WE FOUND IT EMBEDDED IN THE WINGS ON HIS BACK...

WELL, OF COURSE. THE KILLER FIRED FROM THE BALCONY SECTION UP THERE...

THEN THE MURDERER MUST'VE BEEN PRETTY HIGH ABOVE HIM.

JUDGING FROM THE WOUND, THE GUN WAS FIRED DOWNWARD AT AN ANGLE OF 40 DEGREES.

FILE 2:
GOLDEN
APPLE ③

...IS ATHENA, GODDESS OF WISDOM, WHO OFFERED HIM VICTORY IN ALL HIS BATTLES.

THE BRAINY ASIAN-AMERICAN LADY...

...IS HERA, WIFE OF ZEUS AND QUEEN OF THE GODS. SHE PROMISED TO MAKE PARIS RULER OF THE WORLD.

THE RICH TROPHY WIFE...

...IS BASED ON PARIS.

THAT FLASHY ARISTO-CRAT IN THE PLAY...

THE BLONDE SEX-POT IS APHRODITE, GODDESS OF BEAUTY, WHO PROMISED THE PRINCE THE MOST BEAUTIFUL WOMAN IN THE WORLD.

APHRODITE! DUH! ACCORDING TO LEGEND, THAT'S HOW THE TROJAN WAR GOT STARTED.

SO WHO DID THE PRINCE CHOOSE?

IN THIS VERSION OF THE STORY, THE RICH LADY OFFERS THE GUY MONEY, THE SMART LADY OFFERS HIM A GREAT JOB, THE BABE OFFERS HIM A DATE, AND THE GOLDEN APPLE HAS BEEN CHANGED TO A JEWELED APPLE-SHAPED NECKLACE...

AND THE CRABBY LADY WHO GOT MAD AT THE OTHER WOMEN IN THE FIRST SCENE IS BASED ON ERIS, WHO SENT THE GOLDEN APPLE!

...WHEN YOU FIND OUT WHO THE ARISTOCRAT *REALLY* IS...

YOU'RE GOING TO BE SHOCKED...

BUT THIS MUSICAL IS A LITTLE DIFFER-ENT.

IT'S ALL GREEK TO ME.

YOU'D NEVER SEE A PRODUCTION THIS EXTRAVAGANT IN JAPAN!

YOU THINK SO TOO?

THIS IS AMAZING! ♡

YAWN ...

BUT IT LOOKS LIKE *ONE* PHILISTINE DOESN'T AGREE...

SIGH ....

WHAT MYTH IS THAT, MR. KNOW-IT-ALL?

SHEESH... IT'S JUST A FLIMSY ROMANTIC COMEDY RIPPED OFF A GREEK MYTH.

HEY! AREN'T YOU ENJOYING THIS GORGEOUS SHOW?

EACH ONE SECRETLY TRIED TO BRIBE HIM TO CHOOSE HER.

RIGHT. THE THREE GODDESSES DECIDED TO HAVE PARIS, THE PRINCE OF TROY, DECIDE WHICH OF THEM WAS WORTHY OF THE APPLE.

THAT WEIRD GIFT...

...WITH A MESSAGE READING, "FOR THE FAIREST"!

ERIS, THE GODDESS OF DISCORD, WASN'T INVITED, SO SHE GOT JEALOUS AND SENT THEM AN APPLE...

THE JUDGMENT OF PARIS. BASICALLY, THE GODDESSES HERA, ATHENA AND APHRODITE WERE INVITED TO A BIG PARTY.

For the Fairest

HUH?

GOD WOULD NEVER MAKE YOU GO THROUGH THIS.

BUT I'VE GOT BUSINESS ELSE-WHERE...

YES, I WAS PLANNING TO.

WEREN'T YOU GOING TO WATCH THE SHOW WITH US?

HUH?

SEE YOU, VIVIAN. I'M HEADING HOME.

...AND IT LOOKS LIKE A *STORM* IS RISING...

...SO I THINK I'LL PASS.

IT'S OKAY!

YES! THANK YOU SO MUCH FOR SAVING ME!

SHOULDN'T YOU THANK THE *GIRL* INSTEAD?

AAAH...

SEE YOU!

WHOA, WE'VE GOT TO GET READY!

I THINK I'VE GOT A BAND-AID...

HEY, I SCRATCHED MY ARM.

SHF

OW!

SEE? THERE IS NO GOD.

ZHK

CRASH

SOMEBODY'S TRYING TO KILL ME!!

I KNEW IT!

YEAH.

ARE YOU OKAY, RACHEL?

HEY, WHO HUNG THAT HEAVY ARMOR UP THERE?

THE ROPE JUST SNAPPED BECAUSE IT WAS OLD...

YOU WEREN'T SAVED BY GOD OR LUCK.

RIGHT! IT'S OUR LUCKY CHARM!

THANK GOD THE MIRROR WASN'T BROKEN!

BUT SHE'S JUST DROPPING BY WITH HER KIDS, HUH?

WHAT A PITY...

IBLIS HAMILTON (30)

THEY RECEIVED A BOX THREE DAYS AGO.

WEIRD GIFT?

I WAS KIND OF HOPING THE NIGHT BARONESS CAME HERE TO SOLVE THE MYSTERY OF THAT WEIRD GIFT.

...WITH A MESSAGE, "FOR THE FAIREST," WRITTEN IN SOME KIND OF ANIMAL BLOOD.

For the Fairest

INSIDE WAS AN APPLE SPRAY-PAINTED GOLD...

NOW, NOW, MY GODDESSES!

THAT WAS JUST A BAD JOKE!

HEATH FLOCKHEART STAGE ACTOR (33)

I SEE. SO THAT'S WHY THE MOOD IN HERE WAS SO GLUM WHEN WE WALKED IN...

WAH WAH

YES!

THE NIGHT BARONESS!!

ALL THE DEDUCTIONS SHE CAME UP WITH ON THE SHOW TURNED OUT TO BE CORRECT, AND THE CRIMINALS GOT ARRESTED. SO NOW EVERYBODY THINKS SHE'S A **DETECTIVE.**

ONE TIME MOM APPEARED ON SOME AMERICAN REALITY SHOW ABOUT UNSOLVED MYSTERIES.

THAT'S HER NICK-NAME OVER HERE. DAD'S FAMOUS IN THE STATES AS THE AUTHOR OF *NIGHT BARON.*

"NIGHT BARO-NESS"?

BIG DEAL. I BET SHE JUST OVERHEARD DAD MUTTERING STUFF ABOUT THOSE CASES AND REPEATED EVERYTHING HE SAID.

OOH...

HOW CUTE!

?

BUT SHE COULD BE MY **DAUGHTER-IN-LAW** SOMEDAY...

THE BOY IS. THE GIRL ISN'T.

SO ARE THESE YOUR CHILDREN?

I'M SO THRILLED!!

YOU REALLY CAME!

OH, SHARON!

ROSE HEWITT
STAGE ACTRESS (28)

AKANE NEILSON
STAGE ACTRESS (27)

LILA SANCHEZ
STAGE ACTRESS (32)

I GET IT. THIS IS WHEN THEY'VE GOT THEIR STAGE MAKEUP ON AND THEY REALLY LOOK LIKE ACTRESSES.

WAH — WAH

YOU BET IT IS!

OH, IS THAT...?

OF COURSE. THE HEAD OF THIS THEATER GROUP KNOWS SHARON, AND THEY WENT CRAZY WHEN SHE ANNOUNCED SHARON MIGHT BE DROPPING BY.

WOW... THEY'RE ALL SO EXCITED TO SEE SHARON!

YOU ALL KNOW THIS FAMOUS TV SLEUTH...

I KNEW SHE HAD A MORBID SENSE OF HUMOR, BUT THAT WAS CROSSING A LINE!

...DISGUISED PERFECTLY AS *HIM.*

WHEN I WAS PLACING FLOWERS ON MY HUSBAND'S GRAVE, SHE CAME UP BEHIND ME...

THAT LITTLE MINX!

WHAT?

THAT WAS THE LAST TIME I SAW HER. IT'S BEEN ALMOST TEN YEARS.

I THINK SHE FELL IN WITH A *BAD CROWD.*

DIDN'T CHRIS BEG YOU TO TEACH HER ALL YOUR SECRETS OF DISGUISE?

OUR AUDIENCE IS BEGINNING TO CATCH ON THAT THERE'S NO *CAMERA* ROLLING.

WAH WAH

WELL, PARK YOUR CAR. IT'S ABOUT TIME WE WENT BACKSTAGE.

BUT RIGHT BEFORE THE SHOW STARTS ...

DON'T BE SILLY. DURING THE DAY THEY'RE JUST ORDINARY PEOPLE.

WHY'D WE HAVE TO SHOW UP AN HOUR BEFORE THE MUSICAL STARTS? COULDN'T WE HAVE COME BY EARLIER, WHEN THE ACTORS WOULDN'T HAVE BEEN SO BUSY? THEN WE COULD ACTUALLY *TALK* TO THEM.

HEY!

WHAT DID YOU MEAN BY THAT?

THAT'S RIGHT. IT'S JUST BEEN *MISERY* AFTER *MISERY*.

ISN'T THAT RIGHT, SHARON?

SHE'S HAD A TOUGH LIFE!

YOU SAID AN ANGEL NEVER SMILED DOWN ON YOU...

I DON'T SEE HER AS MY DAUGHTER ANYMORE.

OH, COME ON. CHRIS IS YOUR PRIDE AND JOY!

THAT SPOILED DAUGHTER OF MINE HAS NO IDEA WHAT *HARDSHIP* IS. SHE JUST PIGGYBACKED ON THE CAREER I SPENT MY LIFE BUILDING...

AND MY HUSBAND DIED THE DAY AFTER I WON MY OSCAR.

ON THE DAY OF MY SCREEN DEBUT, AFTER STRUGGLING FOR YEARS IN THE BIZ, I LOST BOTH MY PARENTS IN A FIRE.

CASE CLOSED

Volume 35
Shonen Sunday Edition

Story and Art by GOSHO AOYAMA

© 1994 Gosho AOYAMA/Shogakukan
All rights reserved.
Original Japanese edition "MEITANTEI CONAN" published by SHOGAKUKAN Inc.

Translation
Tetsuichiro Miyaki

Touch-up & Lettering
Freeman Wong

Cover & Graphic Design
Andrea Rice

Editor
Shaenon K. Garrity

VP, Production **Alvin Lu**
VP, Sales & Product Marketing **Gonzalo Ferreyra**
VP, Creative **Linda Espinosa**
Publisher **Hyoe Narita**

Printed in Canada

Published by VIZ Media, LLC
P.O. Box 77010
San Francisco, CA 94107

10 9 8 7 6 5 4 3 2 1
First printing, July 2010

SHONEN SUNDAY
SHONENSUNDAY.COM

www.viz.com

Table of Contents

Case Briefing:

Subject:
Occupation:
Special Skills:
Equipment:

Jimmy Kudo, a.k.a. Conan Edogawa
High School Student/Detective
Analytical thinking and deductive reasoning, Soccer
Bow Tie Voice Transmitter, Super Sneakers,
Homing Glasses, Stretchy Suspenders

The subject is hot on the trail of a pair of suspicious men in black when he is attacked from behind and administered a strange substance which physically transforms him into a first grader. When the subject confides in the eccentric inventor Dr. Agasa, they decide to keep the subject's true identity a secret for the safety of everyone around him. Assuming the new identity of first-grader Conan Edogawa, the subject continues to assist the police force on their most baffling cases. The only problem is that most crime-solving professionals won't take a little kid's advice!

CASE CLOSED

VOLUME 35

Gosho Aoyama